INVESTING DESPITE WALL STREET, INC.

Fred Plemenos

McGraw-Hill

NEW YORK   CHICAGO   SAN FRANCISCO
LISBON   LONDON   MADRID   MEXICO CITY
MILAN   NEW DELHI   SAN JUAN   SEOUL
SINGAPORE   SYDNEY   TORONTO

The **McGraw·Hill** Companies

Library of Congress Cataloging-in-Publication Data

Plemenos, Fred.
    Investing despite Wall Street, Inc. / by Fred Plemenos.
       p. cm.
    ISBN 0-07-141525-4 (pbk. : alk. paper)
    1. Stocks—United States. 2. Investment analysis—United States.
3. Investments—United States. I. Title.
HG4910.P53 2003
332.63'22—dc21

                                 2002152447

1 2 3 4 5 6 7 8 9 0 DOC/DOC 0 9 8 7 6 5 4 3

ISBN 0-07-141525-4

This publication is designed to provide accurate and authoritative information in regard to the subject matter covered. It is sold with the understanding that neither the author nor the publisher is engaged in rendering legal, accounting, or other professional service. If legal advice or other expert assistance is required, the services of a competent professional person should be sought.
          —From a declaration of principles jointly adopted by a committee of the
          American Bar Association and a committee of publishers.

 This book is printed on recycled, acid-free paper containing a minimum of 50% recycled de-inked fiber.

McGraw-Hill books are available at special quantity discounts to use as premiums and sales promotions, or for use in corporate training programs. For more information, please write to the Director of Special Sales, Professional Publishing, McGraw-Hill, Two Penn Plaza, New York, NY 10121-2298. Or contact your local bookstore.

Contents

Preface

Warren Buffett's interest in the stock market developed at an early age, stimulated in some measure by frequent visits to his father's office at a local stock brokerage firm. But what has established Buffett as one of the most respected of investors is the success that he has achieved and the reputation that he has cultivated as a no-nonsense investor who closely adheres to the simple investment basics presented by Graham and Dodd in their book *Security Analysis*.

Buffett has become a legend in his own time for good reason—he combines the qualities of being down-to-earth and plain spoken with the attributes of an extremely knowledgeable and dedicated investor. And even more inspiring, he continues to enjoy thoroughly the everyday challenge of what he is doing.

The fascinating part of investing is that it can ignite a lasting and ongoing interest like Buffett's, no matter what a person's age.

The trigger to an individual's initial interest in investing is usually the result of thinking about future financial goals or needs, whether it be retirement, children's college education, a bigger home, or just plain financial independence.

Once an individual begins to think about any of those needs in terms of a real objective, motivation is likely to take care of itself. In many respects, investing takes on the aspects of a continuing adventure. Every new bit of acquired knowledge underscores the fact that there are always new avenues of research or analysis to pursue.

In the late 1990s, however, the time-tested investment principles endorsed and practiced by conventional investors were unceremoniously discarded and replaced by "new-economy" standards and rules of investing.

The catalyst for such a dramatic shift in investment focus was the issuance of several extremely successful initial public offerings (IPOs) that captured investors' imagination.

It did not take Wall Street, Inc. long to exploit the situation, and to popularize the thesis that earnings and P/Es were no longer significant in valuing stocks—especially in the case of "hot" IPO deals that would provide lucrative underwriting fees for the investment bankers. In fact, many of these bankers and their associated analysts assumed the role of primary cheerleaders for these unproven IPO start-up companies that were being touted as having unlimited promise.

Of course, the virtual flood of incredibly successful IPO offerings that followed served to validate that notion.

For investors, the financial community had framed the options as either embracing the future and its promise or being left to languish along with all the "old-economy" stocks.

Wall Street, Inc. unfortunately played its part all too well, causing many ill-prepared individual investors to decide to join the party.

In one particular case, an investor lost about $500,000 investing in a stock recommended by an analyst at a high-profile investment banking firm. Apparently, as the stock declined, he continued to buy more stock on numerous occasions on the basis of the analyst's increasingly enthusiastic "strong buy" ratings. That analyst finally capitulated just days before the company filed for bankruptcy protection.

The real point of that story, however, is the fact that when that investor was asked whether he had conducted any independent research of his own, the answer was no—he had relied entirely on the analyst's advice.

The purpose of this book is to provide the individual with an understanding of the forces that have influenced the stock market under a wide range of market environments, and to establish firmly the process and practices that enhance independent research, analysis, and disciplined investment decision making.

The benefits to an individual investor of acquiring investment knowledge and understanding are not in question—all that is at issue is the matter of deciding to take a meaningful first step in that direction.

Part One

THE HYPE:
HOW WALL STREET, INC.
HYPES STOCKS AND
MOVES MARKETS

1

HOW THE STOCK MARKET REALLY WORKS

I nvesting in the stock market has a simple and beguiling objective—to improve your financial position the easy way by putting your money to work. The concept is enticingly straightforward: Buy the stock of a number of companies or a mutual fund with obviously good prospects and you too will participate in their good fortune.

If only it were as easy as it sounds, even for experienced investors. One need only be reminded of the mania surrounding the Internet bubble of the late 1990s and its aftermath, however, to better understand the reality that the conventional wisdom about stocks and the stock market can sometimes be quite wrong.

How Wall Street Helps Itself, Not You

What happened during that period was aptly and succinctly described by John Bogle, the highly respected founder of the Vanguard group of mutual funds, in a TV interview appearance on *Nightly Business Report* on February 21, 2002, when he stated his belief that the late 1990s period represented a "happy conspiracy of everybody wanting stock prices to go up—CEOs, boards of directors, mutual fund managers, sell-side analysts, buy-side analysts, investment bankers, venture capitalists, and investors—without any regard to valuation." His assessment implies a less than honest and thorough application of what is known as the "prudent man rule," which is assumed to govern the fiduciary responsibility of professional money managers. In fact, that rule was essentially banished from Wall Street's vocabulary and completely ignored because the "new economy" was thought to have rendered it obsolete.

Hype always has been and always will be a factor to be considered in making investment decisions, but it had never previously been as organized, as pervasive, and as matter-of-factly accepted as it was in the 1990s. In that regard, the investment and financial community is truly deserving of the title "Wall Street, Inc." in recognition of its active participation in the unrestrained hyping of stocks and the stock market.

In a telling interview in the April 1, 2002, edition of *BusinessWeek*, Scott McNealy of Sun Microsystems Inc. was asked whether when his company's stock had reached $64 a share 2 years before (Figure 1.1), he had thought it was too good to be true. In answering that question, he made reference to the fact that "2 years ago we were selling at 10 times revenues"

FIGURE 1.1   Sun Microsystems Price Chart

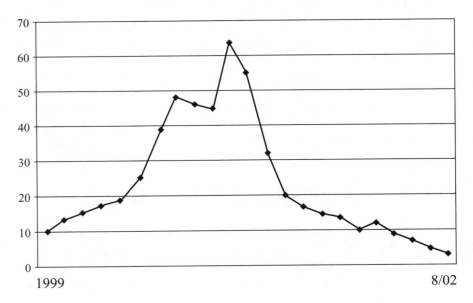

(peak valuation of $207 billion versus peak four-quarter sales of $19.2 billion). He then proceeded to describe the daunting obstacles to providing a meaningful return to investors at that price, and asked a simple question: "Would any of you like to buy my stock at $64?"

Summarizing, he went on to state, "You don't need any transparency. You don't need any footnotes. What were you thinking?" The stock traded as low as $3.50 on August 5, 2002, down 94 percent from its high.

That simple question, "What were you thinking?," represents a fitting metaphor for that bubble period of excess in the stock market—and one that reflects especially badly on Wall Street, Inc.

The glory days of the Internet bubble seemed unstoppable, and Wall Street, Inc. was running at full throttle when I submitted an article entitled "Rationality vs. the Market" to *Barron's* on January 20, 2000, months before the bubble burst. In that article, which *Barron's* chose not to publish, I took notice of a favored tactic of many influential analysts of announcing dramatic increases in their price targets for particular stocks during interviews on the financial news networks like CNBC prior to the opening of the market. These stunning projections were greeted with equally stunning price moves for these and other related stocks, and usually set the tone for the market.

One reason that Sun's stock, like others, continued its meteoric rise was that very practice by stock analysts. The rationale for analysts was quite simple: Since investors obviously were willing to pay more for the stock, it became necessary to follow their lead. Analysts happily participated in and contributed to this incredibly irresponsible charade.

I noted that this practice was contributing to "a market of excesses as analysts compete with each other for bragging rights in this game." I went on to state: "The signs of these excesses, although they are in full view and clearly recognizable, tend to be ignored as rising expectations and the pursuit of superior performance gain momentum."

Market psychology and a strong dose of the greed factor were obviously blinding many investors to the increasing risks. But with many stocks rising 10, 20, 30, and even 50 points in a day, why would one choose not to participate?

I explained my views in that article when I observed:

> Much of the current approach to investing is based on successfully breaking down the old rule barriers that relied on valuation measures such as PEs and dividend yield. Once free of these constraints, investing is limited only by the imagination and creative thinking of both analysts and investors alike.

I will make further reference to that article, but suffice it to say that what was going on was receiving the full and exuberant endorsement of Wall Street, Inc., much to the disservice of many investors who placed their trust in the integrity of the financial community.

In an April 7, 2002, interview carried on the History Channel's "History's Business," Peter Cohen, the former CEO of Shearson Lehman Hutton, characterized what had happened as a "Wall Street–induced boom." This candidly expressed opinion by a former insider clearly and convincingly underscores the fact that the financial community participated in that game of excess, in large measure, for its own self-interest and benefit.

Changes from the "Good Old Days" to the "New Reality" of Today

The old stories about stockbrokers and their yachts may seem quaint today compared to the enormous wealth that was generated in the 1990s by entrepreneurs from their start-up initial public offerings (IPOs). But before the advent of negotiated commission rates on stock transactions, and before the increasing importance of discount brokerage firms (starting in the 1970s) and of the price-advantaged online trading of the 1990s, well-connected stockbrokers had a veritable license to print money.

Even in the early days of negotiated commissions, the trading costs were still very high relative to today's standards. I have some records from 1975 that I saved, basically for sentimental reasons, that illustrate the point. For example, one particular trade indicates a commission of $1150 for trading 5000 shares of a $14 stock in 1975, as opposed to a typical $15 commission today, depending on the type of discount brokerage account you have. In retrospect, it is next to impossible to justify the commission structure of that period, except that the incentive to maintain the status quo was obviously quite high.

The decline in commission rates continued as the discount brokers proliferated, but it was the rapid increase in online trading volume in the mid-1990s that accelerated the move to substantially lower trading costs. As a consequence, the economics of the old brokerage business model changed dramatically during that period, and the brokerage firms had to adjust the way they did business in order to accommodate the new reality.

Predictably, the business model for small brokerage firms could no longer remain viable. In many cases, attempts at combining back-office operations did not work, and starting in the mid-1970s small firms began to either merge or just close down their operations. The consolidation process among small full-service brokerage firms then spread to midsized firms and eventually resulted in mergers and acquisitions involving the larger institutions. The litany of long-gone names of extinct brokerage firms is somewhat reminiscent of the recent dot.com saga.

Charles Schwab was among the first to recognize the changing environment and the potential for discount brokerage firms that could significantly undercut the commissions charged by the large full-service brokerage firms—and individual investors warmed to the concept. But the really crushing blow to the trading commission structure was delivered by the rock-bottom rates charged for Internet online trading accounts. The large full-service brokerage firms, which were burdened by a high-cost personal broker structure, found themselves at an even greater competitive disadvantage, and began suffering declining brokerage revenues and profits.

Since further consolidation between brokerage firms would not fundamentally help the industry's business-model problem, lobbying efforts to seek repeal of the Glass-Steagall legislation of the 1930s began. This was accomplished by the Financial Services Modernization Act of November 12, 1999, which removed limits on activities for banks, insurance companies, and corporations—basically expanding the revenue-generating opportunities of most financial institutions.

Investment banking and underwriting were now essentially wide open, and the creative efforts of Wall Street, Inc. would put together a much more powerful money-making engine than had ever been seen before—and for a while it seemed that the sky was the limit.

The Need for Awareness of Factors That Influence Stock Market Performance

The purpose of this book is not only to add to an investor's fund of knowledge, but also to enhance the investor's awareness of factors that directly or indirectly influence stock market performance.

It is important to note that even very highly regarded money managers have indicated that they finally abandoned their well-established investment principles during the bubble because they felt forced to participate in the action for competitive reasons—in spite of their trepidation. There is an old adage about the stock market that states that critical downturns will come only when all available participants have been lured into the market's trap. The Internet bubble represents a classic example of that cynical view.

While it would seem that the lessons of the late 1990s would be bound to have a lasting impact, there is an almost irresistible tendency for investors to get caught up in even the most transitory of developments that affect a stock or the stock market. The desire to participate in a rising market is obviously tempting—no matter how valid or invalid the rationale for the market's rise.

If one assumes that the late 1990s stock market experience was an aberration, then the question becomes, can we expect the future to be more "normal"? Whatever the answer to that question, however, it goes without saying that an investor who is committing a significant amount of money to the stock market for retirement or other purposes should make a conscious effort to stay as well informed as possible regarding the general economic climate and the factors influencing the prospects of both the stock market in general and individual holdings in particular. In addition, however, the investor must attempt to develop the discipline necessary to protect him- or herself against periods of market psychology that foster risky decision making.

For all intents and purposes, the stock market as we know it today covers approximately a 50-year interval. One certainly cannot dismiss the significance of the 1929 stock market crash and the subsequent impact of the Depression years, but the postwar era that began to pick up speed in the 1950s provides a more meaningful starting point for tracing the evolution of the stock market that exists today.

The Postwar Stock Market: 1950–1995

While the stock market has changed rather dramatically from a structural and operational viewpoint since 1950, the basic underlying forces that characterize the financial community are too deeply ingrained for substantive change. If anything, the power that resides within the Wall Street, Inc. complex has become even more concentrated.

One may wonder how and why the investment community could have so easily ignored and dispensed with well-established investment principles in behaving as it did during the bubble market in the late 1990s. The answer is fairly straightforward: Its members are in business to capitalize on as many opportunities as possible. A review of the Wall Street, Inc. record will serve to make that abundantly clear, and will possibly help the individual investor avoid some of the more obvious pitfalls that seem to continually recur.

The immediate postwar period (1945–1950) was nothing much to brag about. In fact, by 1949 the country was experiencing a counterintuitive stall in economic growth, and the stock market was stuck in the doldrums, having achieved essentially no growth since the end of the war (Figure 1.2).

But the start of the Korean War (June 1950–July 1953) was a clear signal that military spending would be increasing—a factor that helped boost stock prices, with the DJIA rallying from approximately 200 to about 500 by the end of 1955. The 1929 previous high of 375 had finally and permanently been surpassed by the end of 1954—after 25 years!

One of the phrases that had been popular in the financial community was, "What's good for General Motors is good for the country," or words to that effect. But the meaning was clear: What was good for GM would also be good for the stock market. As a corollary, it could be said that the stimulus from military spending would also serve to boost both the economy and the stock market, which would be good for the country—and, indeed, the DJIA performed right on cue on its way to the 1000 level in 1966.

My initial interest in the stock market was sparked in 1954 when I made a Polaroid instant camera marketing presentation for one of my classes. The instant camera was so revolutionary that I knew it would be a great vehicle for my marketing pitch.

Polaroid later became one of the "nifty-fifty" stocks of the early 1970s, but by 2002 it had filed for bankruptcy, a victim of a failed product diversification program and other bad business decisions. Polaroid represents a classic company case study with interesting management and stock market investing issues.

FIGURE 1.2   DJIA Price Chart (1945–1966)

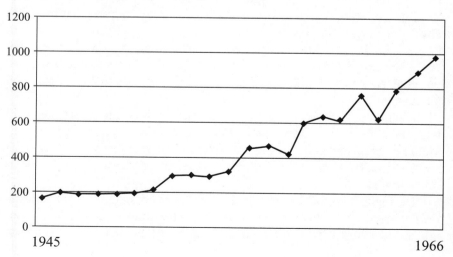

Some Past Examples of Hype

For those who need reminding that stock market hype is an ever-present phenomenon, there is the case of Transitron in the late 1950s. Transitron was one of the first producers of discrete semiconductor diodes, which were experiencing explosive growth for both military and commercial use.

One of my fellow engineering associates who had been investing for a while mentioned that he had bought Transitron at $75 per share and gave me a Merrill Lynch report on the company. My cursory analysis indicated that the stock had soared based on its extremely high profit margin and its perceived dominant competitive position. My concern was that, based on trade information and information gleaned from our engineering contacts related to programs we were working on, semiconductor companies like Texas Instruments and others were quickly gearing up to produce similar devices. As a result, my inclination was that Transitron represented more of a shorting opportunity than a strong buy. But at that point my friend brought in a new Merrill Lynch report that further extolled Transitron's prospects and projected a target price of $125 per share. With Merrill Lynch pushing the stock, even the very thought of shorting seemed foolhardy.

Although Transitron did fleetingly get a bit over $100 per share on the strength of the recommendation, the emergence of bigger and stronger competitors took its toll on Transitron. It quickly declined to $20, and eventually drifted into bankruptcy. I wonder whether the Merrill Lynch analyst wouldn't have recognized the potential problems facing Transitron if his research had been more thorough.

I never forgot that example, which serves as a reminder that hype has always been around—but it didn't always seem so prevalent as it was to become in the late 1990s. The Transitron example makes the case that every investor should examine a company and its industry as extensively as possible, seeking out multiple informed sources for additional information and insight.

Obtaining suitable investment information is a much simpler task today than it was in the 1950s and 1960s. Prior to the computer age, an individual investor depended to a great extent on "market letters" and research reports from brokerage firms as important sources of investment information and ideas.

During that period, I established a number of brokerage accounts just in order to receive the differing viewpoints and the stock selection focus contained in each of their market letters. Unfortunately, that often resulted in calls from various brokers pushing their favorite stock picks—which I rarely agreed with.

An acquaintance who once worked for a prestigious brokerage firm told me of the many occasions on which the office manager would get on the intercom and tell the account executives which stocks they were to push that day. In many cases they would be given sales quotas that had to be met in order to get rid of the firm's inventory in those issues. If a secondary offering were involved, it would be noted that a higher incentive commission would be credited to the broker.

Of course, the concentrated buying pressure induced by these brokers would temporarily push the stock price higher. In effect, the firm's clients had unknowingly artificially bid up the price with their buying—allowing the firm to sell its own inventory at a higher price than would otherwise have been possible. Subsequently, the price would inevitably decline, and it would be up to the account executives to convince their customers that their investment would ultimately prove to be very rewarding.

While that practice smacked of "boiler-room" tactics, the real boiler-room shops generally dealt in the dregs of the over-the-counter (OTC) market. Those firms tended to deal in obscure "penny stocks." High-pressure telephone salespeople at these firms specialized in preying on the gullible, using every trick of the trade in an attempt to elicit a buy order. Fortunately, most of these clearly fraudulent old-style boiler rooms have been driven out of business.

But as the 1990s bubble market demonstrated, the time-tested practices of hype had not been discarded. Rather, the Wall Street, Inc. type of hype was merely being cloaked under a guise of respectability.

The "Nifty-Fifty" Era

The stock market's 16-year tortuous struggle as depicted by Figure 1.3 was exemplified by a DJIA in which several rally attempts from the 600–700 level were not successful in permanently breaking the formidable 1000 barrier. That such a market environment persisted for so long must seem incomprehensible to investors who witnessed the huge gains in the market averages during the 18-year bull-market run from 1982 to 2000.

However, by 1972 a consensus began to emerge that the United States would soon begin to scale down its operations in preparation for a complete withdrawal from Vietnam, and the stock market reacted to that more optimistic outlook by staging a brisk rally that took the DJIA back to the 1000 level later that year. That rally culminated in a phenomenon that gained

FIGURE 1.3   DJIA Price Chart (1966–1982)

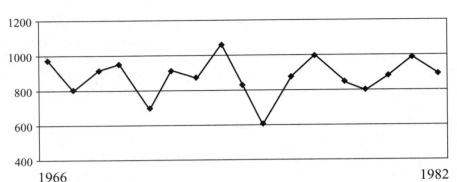

notoriety during 1972, when a relatively small group of stocks given the des-
ignation of the "nifty fifty" achieved valuation levels that seemed to have
risen beyond the realm of reasonableness. If Alan Greenspan had been on
the scene, he might well have deemed it to represent "irrational exuberance."

Much of that "nifty-fifty" mentality developed as the stock market
began to richly reward a group of stocks that had a demonstrated record of
superior income growth. Stocks like Xerox, IBM, and Merck soon attained
the status of glamour growth stocks—and just about every money manager
felt it necessary to own this category of stocks.

Table 1.1 contains a list of 31 NYSE stocks that typified the so-called
nifty fifty in 1972. It is obviously more than sheer coincidence that this list
of high-P/E stocks is dominated by drug, technology, and consumer "franchise" stocks—groups that have historically been generally favored.

P/Es and market valuation levels in billions for both 1972 and 2002 are
also given in Table 1.1. While the current P/E levels for this group of stocks
are significantly lower than the P/E levels in 1972, it should be noted that
many of these companies have experienced a dramatic increase in their
market valuations during the last 30 years.

The story about drug stocks has been fairly compelling, since they have
managed to maintain exceptionally high profit margins over a long period
of time. To a significant extent, this is based on the patent protection that
they enjoy for their successful drugs, which provides them with a lucrative
stream of earnings. Prescription drug growth continues at an inexorable
pace, and the use of these drugs is not considered a matter of choice, nor is
it generally subject to the vagaries of the economy. However, concern about
increasing competitive pressure from generic alternatives for drugs for

TABLE 1.1 "Nifty-Fifty" Stocks

	P/E 1972	P/E 2002	Market Value ($ billions) 1972	Market Value ($ billions) 2002	Market Value Ratio (2002/1972)
Drug Stocks					
Abbott Labs	36	19	1.0	50	50.0
American Home Products (now Wyeth)	36	16	5.5	40	7.2
Bristol Myers	27	10	1.9	43	22.6
Eli Lilly	42	21	4.4	54	12.2
Merck	41	13	5.3	94	17.7
Pfizer	28	20	2.6	175	67.3
Schering-Plough	48	17	3.0	34	11.3
			23.7	490	20.6
Technology Stocks					
Burroughs	46	-	3.5	-	-
Digital Equipment	69	-	0.9	-	-
Electronic Data Systems	59	12	0.7	16	22.8
Emerson Electric	34	25	1.9	21	11.0
General Electric	25	17	12.5	265	21.2
Hewlett-Packard	61	27	1.7	36	21.1
Honeywell	38	38	2.8	25	8.9
IBM	41	25	43.6	119	2.6
Motorola	43	-	1.5	34	22.6
Texas Instruments	50	-	1.8	43	23.9
Xerox	55	-	12.4	4	-
			86.0	563	6.5
Consumer Stocks					
Coca-Cola	45	28	7.8	112	14.3
Disney	79	30	2.5	34	13.6
Eastman Kodak	46	-	20.5	8	-
J. C. Penney	30	38	4.5	4	-
Kresge (S. S.)	46	-	4.4	-	-
McDonald's	81	20	2.2	31	14.1
Pepsico	30	23	1.9	64	33.7
Polaroid	77	-	4.8	-	-
Sears	32	10	18.1	14	-
			74.6	364	4.9
Manufacturing Stocks					
Black & Decker	48	27	1.1	3	2.7
3M	41	30	8.8	42	4.8
Winnebago	80	14	1.1	0.7	-
			11.0	45.7	4.1
TOTALS			**195.3**	**1,462.7**	**7.5**

which patent protection has expired is primarily responsible for the recent decline in the P/E valuations accorded to drug stocks.

The technology sector, which came of age with the advent of computers and semiconductors, is a sector that seems to have attained an almost cultlike following. The pace of innovation in technology far exceeds that in most other areas of business, and it is this dynamic aspect of technology that always seems to offer the prospect of some revolutionary new product or application. The industry as a whole has delivered on its promise of innovation, but business success for individual companies has often been transitory—as the record shows.

Burroughs is one of those cases. As indicated in Table 1.1, in 1972 it had a market capitalization of $3.5 billion and a P/E of 46. It had made the transition from being a leading producer of mechanical adding machines and calculators to being a producer of large mainframe computers. It subsequently merged with Sperry Rand in 1986, and the renamed entity (Unisys) now has a current market valuation of only $2.5 billion. In addition, both Digital Equipment and Xerox failed to fulfill their early promise.

The rather high average P/E accorded to the consumer stocks of the early 1970s listed in Table 1.1 seemed to be based on their "franchise" qualities. While Kresge and Polaroid both went bankrupt, and J. C. Penney and Eastman Kodak have experienced problems, the "franchise" concept remains in vogue today, with the new favorites including Wal-Mart and Home Depot.

As might have been expected, the effort to identify other "nifty-fifty" candidates resulted in a wide-ranging search for "concept" stocks. For example, since a good case could have been made about the bright prospects for pollution control stocks, why shouldn't they have been given special consideration? How about P/Es of 42 for American Air Filter, 54 for Peabody-Galion, or 40 for Wheelabrator-Frye—none of which are still around as independent companies.

Cosmetics distributor Avon apparently seemed to merit a P/E of 62 and a market capitalization of $7.2 billion in 1972, but in 2002 it had a P/E of 26 and a market cap of $11.9 billion, amounting to an average annual appreciation of only 1.7 percent over a 30-year period.

What about the concept of a fast-growing company named Health-Tex, a children's apparel and sleepwear manufacturer, at a P/E of 62? If it had not been acquired long ago, could it possibly have continued to flourish in an import-dominated marketplace?

The idea that housewives would somehow become wildly enthusiastic about sewing their own dresses helped Simplicity Pattern get valued at a

FIGURE 1.4   High and Low P/E Range for the S&P 500 for Eight Periods since 1973

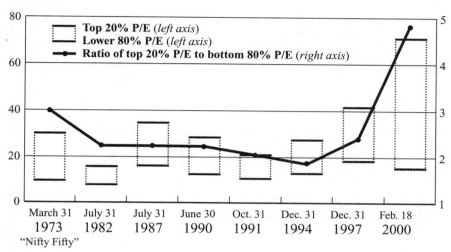

Note: All calculations based on companies in the S&P 500 as the date shown; P/E uses trailing 12-month earnings per share and excludes stocks with negative earnings or unavailable data.
Source: Ned Davis Research Inc.

P/E of 52, but that particular idea did not have staying power. The company eventually faded into oblivion.

As so often happens, the "concept" approach to investing tends to peak during periods of market euphoria.

While the "nifty-fifty" stocks attracted a lot of attention—and notoriety—in the early 1970s, the data presented in Figure 1.4 put that period in somewhat better perspective. A February 24, 2000, *Wall Street Journal* article that was based on data from Ned Davis Research ranks P/Es for the S&P 500 companies and calculates (1) the average P/E of the top 20 percent and (2) the average P/E for the remaining 80 percent. In addition, the chart indicates the ratio of those two values. It appears that the valuation excesses of the stock market in the late 1990s have handily exceeded the valuations of that much-maligned "nifty-fifty" era.

The Conglomerate Fad

Another episode of note during this interval concerned the conglomerate fad of the late 1960s and early 1970s. The basic premise was that companies with a diversified business portfolio would tend to provide superior performance across business cycles. This concept was widely promoted by high-powered consulting firms and investment bankers, who collected handsome fees for helping to put all the pieces together.

Unfortunately, the theory fell victim to real-world problems. To begin with, the original idea was that the ideal conglomerate should be a balanced combination of "cash cow" business units, growth units, countercyclical units, and so on. But in practice, acquisition deals were often arranged in a less organized way as targets of opportunity presented themselves. And once these disparate businesses with their varied management cultures had been acquired, their integration turned out to be more challenging than had been anticipated.

Who can remember the formerly prominent conglomerates like Gulf & Western Industries, which was facetiously referred to as "Engulf & Devour"? Or does anybody remember the likes of long-gone entities such as A-T-O Inc., Fuqua Industries, Rapid-American Corp., and Questor Corp.?

The Explosive Growth of Mutual Funds

The influence of Wall Street, Inc. on market activity during the early 1970s "nifty-fifty" period was quite evident. But that influence was to get even more noticeable as a result of the rapid growth of mutual funds from the 100 to 200 level during the 1960s and 1970s to an estimated 8000 by the end of the century.

Much of that explosive growth came after the passage of the 401(k) legislation in 1984. In effect, that legislation marked the shift in emphasis of retirement programs from corporate defined-benefit plans to individual defined-contribution plans, whose assets now approximate $2 trillion.

One major advantage of 401(k) plans is that the individual owns these tax-deferred assets, and so they are portable from one employer to another, unlike corporate pension plans, which have strict vesting requirements and sharply reduced benefits if the employee leaves the company before prescribed conditions are met.

There can be little doubt that the growth of 401(k) accounts has contributed to the proliferation of mutual funds, and has provided the funds with what has been a fairly consistent flow of money that has to be continually invested.

One implication of the increasing dominance of mutual funds is that they now are in a relatively powerful position to influence investment trends. The investment decision making of just a few dozen managers of the largest funds can set the tone regarding market-moving sector rotation as well as overall market direction.

That obvious conclusion is supported by stock trading data. When stock market moves on a given day were propelled by 100 million share trading volumes for high fliers like Intel and Cisco, while the majority of other stocks traded their usual 10,000 to 50,000 shares, there is no doubt about where the buying or selling pressure was coming from.

Many fund managers admit that they will buy a stock only when it has received multiple brokerage upgrades, thereby assuring general institutional buying pressure. That investment rationale, based on analysts' recommendations, along with sponsorship considerations and momentum, trumps other, more fundamental, considerations.

The 1973–1974 Stock Market Collapse

For a while it seemed that the "nifty-fifty" market that had pushed the DJIA back to the 1000 level might represent the beginning of a breakout move, but the market was soon to be seriously jolted.

The Senate vote on February 7, 1973, to investigate Watergate had begun to undermine investor psychology, but it was the Yom Kippur War, which started on October 5, 1973, and resulted in the Arab oil embargo to nations supporting Israel, that provided the crushing blow to investor confidence.

There was a 6-month period in 1974 during which the market declined day after day with essentially no respite. There were literally no safe havens, and the DJIA sank to approximately 575 in a stock market collapse that was extremely traumatic by any standard.

From a low of 570 in the DJIA in December 1974, the stock market staged a remarkable recovery to the 900 level in 1975, and it peaked at 1026 in September 1976. This represented a fairly predictable reaction to a developing economic recovery from a fairly deep recession.

Technology and NASDAQ Signal a Changing Market

To a large extent, the stock market began to move into a new era starting in 1975. By that time, the NASDAQ market, which had been established in 1971 to centralize what had been a highly fragmented over-the-counter market, began to take shape.

In addition, the technology sector was on the verge of very substantial product development breakthroughs. For example, the introduction of very large-scale integrated circuits had made it possible for companies like Digital Equipment, Data General, Prime Computer, and Wang Labs to develop minicomputers that challenged the dominance of large mainframe computers. The growing acceptance of these products served to provide exceptional growth for these companies well into the 1980s.

At one time, Prime Computer was held in such high esteem that its stock price was considered to be a market bellwether—again, it was a case of "as Prime Computer goes, so goes the market." But ultimately all of these companies succumbed to fierce competitive pressures and technological change.

At the height of its success, Digital Equipment employed approximately 130,000 people, and its chairman expressed the belief that Digital could grow enough to produce the entire world's demand for minicomputers. However, Digital missed the PC transition and was subsequently acquired by Compaq Computer—which in turn has been acquired by Hewlett-Packard.

It should be acknowledged, however, that during their high-flying days, these companies provided outstanding investment returns. Timing, as always, makes a big difference, as the Internet bubble of the 1990s makes abundantly clear. The fact that most of the early entrants into the computer field have not prospered or even survived is testament to the difficulty in making long-term investment projections with any degree of confidence.

How can 10- to 15-year cash flow projections by analysts be taken seriously as a basis for placing a value on a given stock when the very survival of so many companies has come into question over the years?

The First Phase of the Bull Market: 1982–1987

It is generally accepted that investors are most vulnerable to hype during periods of rising optimism about the stock market. Conversely, when markets are in decline, the tendency is for investors to basically avoid the stock market.

In many respects, the investment environment from 1976 to 1982 had not been conducive to much risk taking. The economic problems, which included rising oil prices and a high inflation rate, seemed intractable, and with money market yields having reached 18 percent at the end of this period, there was no amount of hype that could possibly overcome the despair that investors were experiencing.

But in August 1982, all that despair on the part of investors gave way to jubilation. An impending financial crisis created by Mexico's threatened default on $60 billion of foreign debt was averted by a huge bailout by the U.S. government, and the Federal Reserve simultaneously began to lower interest rates. The bull market was on its way, and Wall Street, Inc. would not have long to wait for better times and bigger opportunities.

One possible explanation of the market's behavior after the 1982 recession shown in Figure 1.5 may be found in the data contained in Figure 1.6. The P/E for the S&P 500 had ranged between 15 and 20 over the entire decade of the 1960s, only to decline abruptly as interest rates rose in the 1970s and early 1980s. Figure 1.6, which examines the P/Es for high-growth, moderate-growth, and average-growth sectors and for the S&P 500 as a whole (solid line), provides compelling evidence that P/E levels had established an almost impenetrable 10-year base.

If P/E levels were to go no lower, the obvious conclusion would be that, barring some unanticipated shock, the market would trade higher in response to improving corporate earnings and expanding P/E levels.

For all intents and purposes, then, it was ultimately the combination of relatively low initial valuation levels and a more accommodating Federal Reserve that served to override general concerns about mundane issues such as deficits and debts. Once again, the Federal Reserve had demonstrated that it can be either the boon or the bane of the stock market.

The euphoria induced by a series of further significant rate cuts over the 1984–1986 period helped the stock market mount a broad rally that

FIGURE 1.5   DJIA Price Chart (1982–1992)

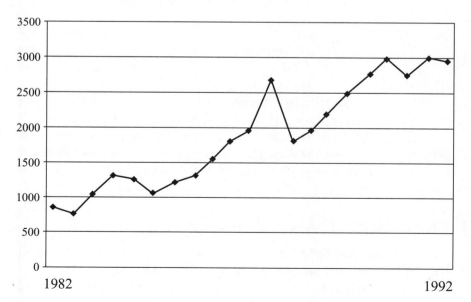

FIGURE 1.6   P/E for the S&P 500 versus Industry Sectors with High, Moderate, and Average Income Growth

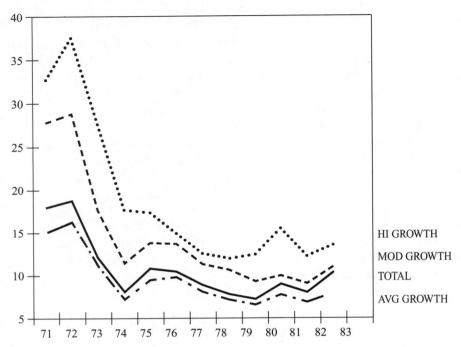

drove the DJIA to a series of record new highs, finally reaching a 1987 "pre-crash" level of 2700. Much of that gain was fueled by an expansion of the P/E for the S&P 500 to 23, representing a return to the 1960s level (Figure 1.7).

The obvious question that presents itself is the reasons behind the S&P 500 valuation surge from P/Es of 7 to 8 to approximately the 23 level. Strategists were quick to explain that the market was just making up the ground that had been lost during previous years of stock market underperformance. The logic apparently suggests that it takes overvaluation to compensate for past periods of undervaluation.

The 1987 Market Crash and the Influence of Program Trading

The expansive mood that had permeated Wall Street from the beginning of the year was unceremoniously jolted on October 19, 1987 (Black Monday), when the DJIA plunged 508 points (−22.6 percent), the greatest

FIGURE 1.7   S&P 500 P/E Ratio (1926–2001)

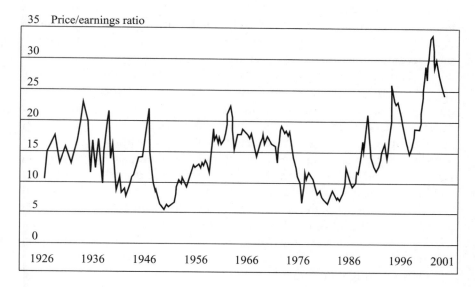

one-day stock market percentage loss in history. While stock market analysts differ on the reason for that event, two prominent causes were

1.   Computerized "program" trading tied to index futures and other
      derivative trading by large institutions
2.   Overvaluation

Both factors did, indeed, contribute to the severity of the crash. Large
institutions had carefully honed their "program trading" operations, so that
with one click of their computer keyboard, they could, for example, execute
simultaneous buy and sell orders for a "basket of stocks" on the one hand,
and S&P 500 futures contracts on the other.

Most Wall Street firms had hired theoretical mathematicians with
advanced degrees to help develop these and other trading strategies. The
impact of these programs on day-to-day trading became very evident in the
form of sudden, but otherwise inexplicable, price moves in both stocks and
the averages. These artificial gyrations proved rather unsettling for many,
especially for individual investors. For the institutional traders, however,
the strategy was successful in providing a seemingly riskless but profitable
return, and institutions became very comfortable with the apparent inherent safety of program trading based on their experience up to that time.

However, those wonderfully precise theoretical program trading models would soon be put to an unanticipated real-world test. In reconstructing the events that contributed to the Black Monday meltdown, stories surfaced that Fidelity fund managers had begun to sell during the preceding week as they became concerned about extended valuations in the market. As their concerns deepened over the weekend before Black Monday, they reportedly decided to unwind some existing positions. But that attempt was quickly detected by other large institutions, resulting in additional sell orders, which created a significant order imbalance at the opening. Without the benefit of the trading curbs or temporary halts to trading that were subsequently put in place, the massacre continued unabated that day. While the DJIA managed to establish a strong technical base over the next year, it would take 2 years—until October 1989—for the 1987 high to be surpassed.

The 1987 crash highlights an important aspect of the new face of the stock market. The indisputable linkage of that event to institutional program trading raises a question regarding the underlying benefit derived from this activity.

One clue might be found in the fact that during several weeks in mid-2002, up to 43 percent of the NYSE's daily trading volume was ascribed to program trading. Certainly, from the perspective of the brokerage community, that business is a very important part of total trading commissions. In addition, the associated trading in futures, options, and other index derivatives also benefits the bottom line. It is not surprising, then, that the financial community continues to invent an increasing number of financial instruments of all kinds.

For the most part, this is all an inside game, played by institutions. Investors are relegated to the sidelines as passive observers of the huge trading volume that occurs on futures and option expiration dates. Since the leverage in these instruments can be immense, there can be very significant returns for professional traders if the underlying stocks can be nudged in the right direction just before those instruments expire.

This type of last-minute trading could be viewed as manipulation, but it is a kind of manipulation that is openly practiced by the large institutions, so it must be okay. Once again, this is not a game that individual investors can play.

Wall Street, Inc. Discovers Biotechnology

In the late 1980s and early 1990s, Wall Street, Inc. found a new concept to run with—biotechnology. The story had all the important attributes necessary to attract the interest of investors.

For starters, a number of pioneering biotechnology companies, such as Genentech and Amgen, were involved in research programs that were beginning to yield the promise of important pharmaceutical products.

The very thought of discovering an anticancer drug is often enough to generate a significant level of investor enthusiasm. I recall watching the trading action on one of the early financial news programs; Amgen's symbol, AMGN, was "painting the tape," with prices ticking up with each posted trade.

It did not take Wall Street, Inc. long to figure out that there might be many other opportunities like Amgen to be exploited. As happened later with Internet-related stocks, the investment bankers sought out researchers in the field and quickly arranged hundreds of IPOs for start-up companies that planned to expand their research into "promising" therapeutical drugs. Each successful IPO would, of course, be followed by the obligatory glowing research report from the underwriting firm's analyst. Unfortunately, the drug discovery process can take many years, and it often ultimately results in failure. In the meantime, these biotech companies are burdened with the need to meet payrolls and pay for very expensive approval trials before they ever receive any revenues.

The high "cash-burn" rates that characterize biotech firms guarantee that all but a few of them are in constant need of new debt or equity financing. The majority of those hundreds of start-up biotech firms eventually folded or have just continued to languish.

Wall Street, Inc., however, had done its job and was on the lookout for the next good concept. An interesting follow-up concerning the biotech field is that during the Internet bubble market, a renewed interest in the field was sparked by news that the effort to map the human genome was nearing completion. While this development could not have been expected to generate meaningful revenues for some time, the hype machine got busy on this new version of the biotech story. After a brief but powerful rally in the group, however, interest in these stocks virtually disappeared, like interest in other speculative groups.

The important fact to keep in mind is that Wall Street, Inc. makes its money primarily from brokerage commissions and from underwriting fees for IPOs and other offerings. The significance of those profits can be gauged by the size of the annual compensation packages that these investment banking firms paid to their "star" analysts in the 1990s—$15 to $25 million in some cases. Obviously these firms recognized the value of hype in stimulating investor interest. When the financial incentives are powerful enough, it can be expected that ethical behavior will be shaded and that well-established investment principles will conveniently be ignored or somehow explained away.

In 1995 the economy seemed to be going in the right direction, and that increasing optimism was to be reflected in what turned out to be a huge and extended bull-market run in stocks. The wonderful stock market ride would soon be a matter of technology, technology, and more technology.

2

THE STOCK MARKET BUBBLE OF THE LATE 1990S

The Internet Transformed Everything

You don't need Webster's dictionary to define euphoria—NAS-DAQ's 86 percent gain in 1999 (Figure 2.1) clearly conveys the meaning. Webster's calls euphoria "a feeling of well-being or elation," but what was happening in the stock market went far beyond that. In retrospect, one would have to go all the way through the entire dictionary to the letter *z* to find the appropriate word—"zaniness," which Webster's defines as "fantastically or absurdly ludicrous."

There is no denying the favorable fundamentals that were developing for the technology sector by the mid-1990s. The real disconnect, however, arose as so-called visionaries began to extrapolate future prospects with excessive zeal and hype. The most egregious of these assumptions were focused on the premise that the Internet and the dot.com companies were going to dominate the world of commerce at the expense of the "old economy"—it was to be a question of "clicks versus bricks."

FIGURE 2.1   NASDAQ Price Chart (1995–August 2002)

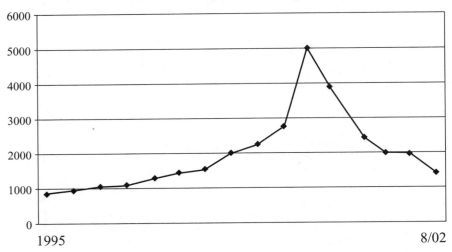

As Table 2.1 reveals, those rising expectations produced incredible 5-year compound rates of return for all the major market indices, including the S&P 500 (Figure 2.2) and the DJIA (Figure 2.3), but the postbubble market correction substantially reduced those percentage gains when measured over a $7^1/_2$-year interval (January 1995 to August 2002). In effect, one of the most spectacular bull markets that had produced parabolic price increases had reached valuation levels that not even the most bullish of analysts could coax higher.

There is little question that the Internet can be looked upon as both a remarkable innovation and a technological marvel. As such, it was able to capture the imagination and set in motion a virtual tidal wave of enthusiasm.

During the bubble phase, the term *transforming* was used to describe the potential impact of the Internet. In the process, the focus was shifted from the realities of the Internet business models to a stock market phenomenon with all the excesses that one can conjure up.

From the telcos that were going to wire up the whole world over land, sea, and air, to fiber-optic companies, to hardware and software companies and consultants, to storage-farm companies, and of course all the dot.com companies that were going to put everybody else out of business in the "new-economy" revolution—there was no apparent limit to the opportunities. The Internet was indeed viewed as a gigantic transforming force.

While the PC had also been considered a transforming force, it had been transformed into a commodity product that was confronted by fierce com-

TABLE 2.1   Compound Gains for the Major Market Indices

	5-Year Compound Gain (1/95–2/00)	$7^{1}/_{2}$-Year Compound Gain (1/95–8/02)
DJIA	24.0%	10.3%
S&P 500	29.0%	9.6%
NASDAQ	46.5%	6.6%

FIGURE 2.2   S&P 500 Price Chart (1995–August 2002)

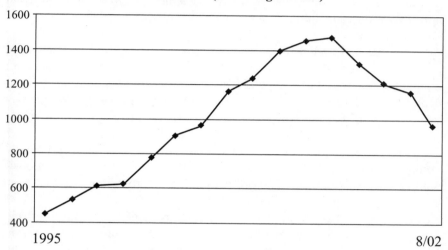

FIGURE 2.3   DJIA Price Chart (1995–August 2002)

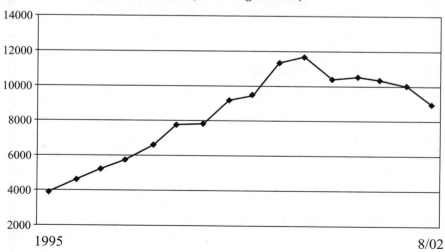

petitive pressures—but the Internet seemed destined to transcend any such difficulties.

In the mid-1990s PCs were, in fact, gaining momentum, helped in large measure by the growing attraction of the Internet, which had become the best story in town. In the view of "visionaries," the Internet revolution represented the opportunity of a lifetime, helping to create an environment of "anything goes"—which turned out to be quite contagious. As the price of Internet-related stocks soared beyond reason, even previously rational investors began to feel that they were losing by not winning at what appeared to be a sure thing—even though the market had taken on the attributes of a casino.

The real and undeniable benefits that flowed from the Internet were soon to be essentially overwhelmed by the wild proliferation of dot.com companies that were brought public on the basis of nothing more than a concept. The dot.com episode was a travesty at best, as entrepreneurs, aided by venture capitalists and investment bankers, behaved with a shocking disregard for the most basic of business and financial principles.

For Wall Street, Inc., it was like a dream come true as the flood of IPO commissions enriched their coffers. But that extremely lucrative IPO business faded just as fast as the more than 500 dot.com companies that have either ceased operations or gone bankrupt.

The Internet has been transforming in many respects, but far less so in others. Undoubtedly the novelty has worn off. Most individual users no longer feel compelled to be online for hours at a time either chatting or idly surfing the Net. And businesses no longer feel the pressure to fend off a possible clicks versus bricks onslaught. The old economy basically continues to function as it did before, and the mall retailers, supermarket chains, and auto dealers have retained their dominance as far as the consumer is concerned. Efficiencies have certainly been implemented in many areas of business operations, but to the outsider the changes are not very noticeable.

It may be some time before another transforming development is anointed by Wall Street, but when it is, it should be subjected to a healthy dose of scrutiny and a disciplined and realistic assessment of its claims and assumptions. For example, there already is a low-level drumbeat about the impact of an "Internet II" that will be bigger and better than the last version. Be prepared.

The great market ride experienced by market participants during the period from 1995 to 2000 was predicated in large measure on a widespread belief that the rules of investing had radically changed. But the basic rules of investing can't be that easily repealed—they had only been temporarily and mistakenly suspended. The following sections examine several distinct characteristics of that period, concentrating not only on what happened, but on how and why things got so out of control during that great ride.

The Magic Carpet—Woven by the PC, Telecom, and the Internet

It is very rare indeed for so many elements to fall into place as perfectly as they did for technology in the mid-1990s. PC penetration was beginning to kick into high gear in both the business and consumer markets as a result of rapidly improving performance capabilities and decreasing prices. More powerful PCs, of course, were made possible by the steady stream of faster and smaller semiconductor devices.

The idea of the Internet had been funded and pursued by the military's Advanced Research Projects Agency (ARPA), resulting in the implementation of a limited prototype called ARPANET in 1967. But the Internet as it exists today was made practical by the more recent development of the high-performance and cost-effective hardware and software that made it commercially viable.

The Internet's complex data transmission system is composed of broad-band switches, routers and fiber-optic cables and equipment, while its ability to support data access for the growing Web site universe required a large and expanding memory storage capacity. All these developments had seemed to come together as if it had been planned that way. At the time, industry and stock market participants could not believe their extraordinary good fortune—the experience seemed akin to being on a magic carpet ride. But the magic would be gone all too soon.

The Internet came to be accepted as a transforming development as it became clear that the capability existed to make it a reality, and that perception unleashed a new wave of technological innovation and product development. The result was one of those virtuous cycles in which the initial growth phase stimulates a higher level of demand, resulting in more product enhancement, then more growth, and so on.

The Telecommunications Act of 1996 (February 8, 1996) was, in retrospect, a major contributor to the Internet bubble. It stated:

> The goal of this new law is to let anyone enter any communications business—to let any communications business compete in any market against any other.

Unfortunately, the grand vision expressed by that deregulation legislation ultimately degenerated into what has been referred to as a debacle.

Some of the early expectations regarding the Internet's growth potential were predicated on subscribers having access not only to the relatively slow dial-up connections, but also to either the much faster digital subscriber lines (DSL) or broadband cable's high-speed modems.

Once the 1996 Telecommunications Act had made it possible for any and all to participate in that business, scores of new start-ups entered the telecom marketplace as competitive local exchange carriers (CLECs), pitting themselves against the long-established "incumbent" carriers. Competition is often considered a good thing, but this was to become a case of too much of a good thing.

The incumbent carriers responded to the perceived competitive threat from CLECs and other Internet service providers (ISPs) by embarking on their own heavy spending on data and voice networks. The CLECs, flush with the money raised from their IPOs, rushed to establish a competitive advantage in chosen markets. This heavy up-front capital spending outpaced revenues by a wide margin, and brutal competition eliminated any prospect of generating meaningful profits that could sustain the CLECs' ambitious capital spending plans.

Basically, then, the technology sector had fed off the demand that had been generated by telecom-related spending, which included spending on networking equipment for routing Internet traffic, computers and servers for servicing Web sites, and the fiber-optic systems for data transmission lines. All of this potential demand obviously augured well for the technology sector—and the prospect of an ever-expanding market had captured the imagination of investors, venture capitalists, and investment bankers alike.

However, the CLECs were digging a big hole for themselves. They needed a steady infusion of new capital in order to keep operating. Wall Street, Inc. willingly lent a helping hand by arranging new debt financing.

One does not need the benefit of hindsight to question the judgment of those professional money managers who bought huge amounts of telecom bonds, nor that of the large investment banks that retained positions in syndicated telecom bank loans. This financing certainly was based not on careful consideration of the financial qualifications of the borrower, but rather on the vaguely outlined promise of the industry's phenomenal growth prospects. In the final analysis, it was the easy and unfettered access to the capital markets that fueled the excesses that were developing.

When all was said and done, an estimated $1.4 trillion had been spent on telecom-related projects. It had been a boon for the financial community, generating record-setting underwriting fees along with huge bonuses for the cheerleading analysts. While much of that spending would ultimately be shown to have been wasteful and ill-founded, it created a bonanza for many technology companies while it lasted.

Among the beneficiaries were companies like Dell, Gateway, and Hewlett-Packard, whose performance reflected the strong demand for PCs, while EMC's memory systems filled the demand coming from the Web-hosting needs of the Internet.

A review of Dell's 5-year price performance shows that the stock rose from about $5 per share in early 1997 to almost $60 in early 2000, valuing Dell at a P/E of 73 and a market cap of $156 billion. These numbers represent a rather substantial premium over Dell's January 2002 book value of $1.80 and stockholders' equity amounting to $4.7 billion.

An even more explosive pattern developed for EMC. EMC's peak price of $105 per share occurred in the summer of 2000, resulting in a P/E of 128 and a market value of $232 billion, compared to a book value of $3.47 per share and stockholders' equity of $7.6 billion.

But the most prominent technology company of that period surely had to be Cisco (Figure 2.4). At its peak price of $82 per share, Cisco's P/E was an astounding 227, and its market value was a cool $600 billion (approximating the market value of the entire NYSE at its 1982 low).

FIGURE 2.4   Cisco Price Chart

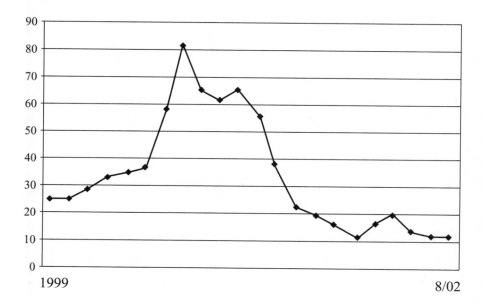

1999   8/02

It is beyond comprehension that investors could have been so taken in by the hype and mystique that was generated by the constant drumbeat for Cisco emanating from Wall Street, Inc. When Cisco would beat analysts' estimates for quarterly earnings by a penny, the analysts and fund managers who appeared on financial programs like CNBC would become even more effusive about Cisco's prospects, and Cisco's stock would jump in after-hours trading, setting the tone for even higher overall stock market gains the next day.

Cisco's highest quarterly EPS amounted to $0.11 per share, and its record high fiscal 2000 EPS amounted to all of $0.36 per share. For the 5 fiscal years ending in July 2001, Cisco's total earnings amounted to $6.2 billion, or $0.85 per currently outstanding share (an average annual EPS of $0.17)—obviously an awe-inspiring number for all the uninhibited bull enthusiasts who "believed."

JDS Uniphase Corp. (Figure 2.5) was another "darling" of Wall Street that had embarked on a very expensive acquisition expedition in the hope of dominating the fiber-optic equipment sector—but unfortunately, JDSU was forced to write off over $50 billion in acquisition-related goodwill.

A selected group of 22 high-profile companies in the computer, software, Internet infrastructure, semiconductor, telecom, and contract manufacturing sectors is given in Table 2.2. The peak market value of each company in billions (column 1) is based on the stock's highest price, indicated in column 2. The total peak market capitalization of these 22 compa-

FIGURE 2.5   JDS Uniphase Price Chart

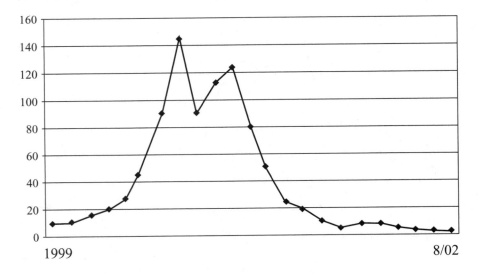

TABLE 2.2   Peak Valuation Data for 22 Technology Stocks

	(1) Peak Market Cap ($ billions)	(2) High Price	(3) 2001 Income ($ millions)
Computer-Related Stocks			
Dell Computer	156	60	1,246
EMC Corp.	232	105	(507)
Gateway Inc.	27	84	(1,014)
Hewlett-Packard	152	78	408
IBM	239	139	7,723
	806		
Software Stocks			
Microsoft	650	120	7,346
Oracle	255	46	2,561
	905		
Internet Infrastructure Stocks			
Ciena Corp.	50	151	(1,794)
Cisco Systems	600	82	(1,014)
Corning Inc.	107	113	(5,498)
JDS Uniphase	208	153	(5,379)[*]
Lucent Technologies	288	84	(4,013)[*]
Nortel Networks	285	89	(27,302)
	1,538		
Semiconductor-Related Stocks			
Applied Materials	94	115	775
Broadcom Corp.	74	275	(2,742)
Intel Corp.	508	76	1,291
PMC-Sierra	42	256	(639)
Qualcom Inc.	153	200	(549)
Texas Instruments	173	100	(201)
	1,044		
Telecome/Wireless/Contract Mfg.			
Motorola Inc.	140	61	(3,937)
Nokia	293	63	1,961
Solectron	40	53	(124)
	473		(56,674)
TOTALS	**4,766**		**(116,674)[*]**

[*] With charges

nies rose to an astounding $4.77 trillion—or about a third of the estimated $15 trillion peak valuation of all traded stocks at the time.

The stock market is often cited as purportedly serving an important role as a discounting mechanism, but based on the $56.7 billion operating loss reported by these companies for 2001 (column 3), the market had clearly failed in that capacity.

A number of the companies listed in Table 2.2 experienced particularly large losses, and some former high fliers like Ciena, Corning, Lucent, and Nortel are now struggling to remain viable.

The outsourcing contract manufacturing giant Solectron is interesting in that it represents a good proxy for the technology sector. Many technology companies have, to a very large extent, adopted outsourcing policies in order to reduce costs. As a consequence, Solectron's revenue trend could provide early indications of any impending improvement in the production levels of the technology sector.

While the magic carpet ride was basically a technology story, it became an even bigger stock market story.

Starting in 1995, the DJIA (Figure 2.3) went on to establish an impressive record, breaking each thousand-point barrier (Table 2.3) with unprecedented speed through the April 1999 breaching of the 11,000 level. Those had indeed been days characterized by giddy enthusiasm and high expectations.

What is interesting about the strong performance of the DJIA over the 1995–1999 period is that this price-weighted index, consisting of just 30 stocks, did not seem to have the heavy tech weighting that boosted the S&P 500 and propelled NASDAQ. Nevertheless the more traditional group of DJIA stocks did seem to be experiencing some measure of the froth engendered by the NASDAQ "new-economy" fever. This phenomenon is captured by the data in column 4 of Table 2.4, indicating the large percentage declines experienced by the 30 DJIA stocks from their 5-year peak prices (column 2) to their August 2, 2002, price levels (column 3).

TABLE 2.3   Breaking the DJIA Thousand-Point Barriers

DJIA	Date	Elapsed Time in Months
2,000	1/87	
3,000	4/91	39
4,000	2/95	46
5,000	11/95	9
6,000	10/96	11
7,000	2/97	4
8,000	7/97	5
9,000	4/98	9
10,000	3/99	11
11,000	4/99	1
12,000	?	40[*]

[*] As of August 2002.

TABLE 2.4   Market Price Performance Data for DJIA Stocks (Ranked by 8/2/02 Market Capitalization)

	(1) Market Cap ($ billions)	(2) Peak Price	(3) 8/2/02 Price	(4) % Change	(5) P/E
1. General Electric	294	60	29	−52	19.4
2. Microsoft	241	120	44	−63	31.5
3. ExxonMobil	228	47	34	−28	22.3
4. Wal-Mart	205	69	46	−37	29.7
5. Citigroup	159	58	31	−47	10.6
6. Johnson & Johnson	157	65	52	−29	28.4
7. Coca-Cola	124	87	50	−42	30.5
8. Procter & Gamble	117	116	90	−22	40.1
9. IBM	116	138	68	−51	23.2
10. Intel	112	75	17	−77	55.7
	1753				
11. Merck	108	95	48	−49	15.3
12. Philip Morris	97	58	45	−22	10.4
13. SBC Communications	92	58	27	−53	13.5
14. Home Depot	67	68	28	−59	20.6
15. J. P. Morgan	48	66	24	−64	33.6
16. 3M	47	130	120	−8	28.1
17. American Express	44	62	33	−47	23.4
18. DuPont	39	82	39	−52	8.0
19. Hewlett-Packard	38	64	13	−80	27.8
20. AT&T	35	47	9	−81	—
	615				
21. Boeing	32	70	40	−43	15.2
22. Disney	31	43	15	−65	28.4
23. United Technologies	31	87	65	−25	16.6
24. McDonald's	30	48	24	−50	18.4
25. Honeywell	26	67	30	−55	38.4
26. General Motors	24	93	43	−54	13.5
27. Alcoa	22	45	25	−45	35.4
28. International Paper	18	60	38	−37	—
29. Caterpillar	14	65	42	−35	22.1
30. Eastman Kodak	9	88	29	−67	—
	236				
TOTAL	**2,604**				

While it is true that there were four pure technology stocks in the DJIA (Microsoft, Intel, IBM, and Hewlett-Packard), it seems that the overall peak price levels achieved by the Dow stocks during the bubble phase of the stock market were based on the general stock market mood, which expected ever-higher stock prices and annual returns in the 20 to 30 percent range—independent of valuation considerations. How else could the robust peak price levels indicated in column 2 for stocks like Coca-Cola ($87) and Disney ($43) have been justified at a time when their earnings records, listed in Table 2.5, were so uninspiring?

In contrast to the DJIA, both the S&P 500 and NASDAQ are market-capitalization-weighted indices, which tends to exacerbate the contribution of the large number of highly valued tech stocks that are part of these indices.

A large majority of investors still consider the concept of P/E somewhat relevant as one of the factors to consider when making an investment decision, and it would be natural to expect that a P/E measure would be available for the market indices as well. However, that is not the case for NASDAQ.

Calculating an average P/E for a group of companies will result in distortions if only the positive P/Es are averaged and companies with earnings losses or negligible earnings are excluded from the calculation. The correct methodology consists of a simple calculation that divides the sum of all market values by the summed total income (with total negative incomes subtracted from total positive incomes), as indicated by

$$P/E = \frac{\text{market capitalization total}}{\text{combined total income}}$$

This calculation can be easily performed in this modern computer age, but NASDAQ conspicuously avoids it. Obviously, with so many NASDAQ-listed companies experiencing losses rather than profits, the calculated P/E would be quite embarrassing—and so it is never made available as an official number. As a consequence, investors are left with only rough estimates, which are sometimes quoted as being approximately 200.

However, one need only scan the P/E columns in the *Wall Street Journal* to get an idea of how horrendous the P/E for NASDAQ would probably be. The P/E columns for the NASDAQ listings are dominated by two notations:

(dd) Loss in the most recent four quarters

(cc) P/E ratio is 100 or more

Table 2.5   5-Year EPS Record for Coca-Cola and Disney

	Coca-Cola	Disney
1997	1.64	0.95
1998	1.42	0.89
1999	0.98	0.62
2000	0.88	0.57
2001	1.60	0.11

But the reality of meager earnings or losses for a large majority of NAS-DAQ stocks apparently did not deter Wall Street, Inc. from pushing, touting, and otherwise beating the drums for the next batch of speculative IPOs that would add more money-losing companies to the list.

Everybody Is Getting Rich

As Figures 2.1, 2.2, and 2.3 indicate, the broad markets were in a very solid uptrend over the 1995–2000 period. But it was the performance of NAS-DAQ over the 15-month interval that started in the fall of 1998 and ended in the spring of 2000 that made the headlines. That move was of truly unprecedented proportions, and it gained momentum as it went along, resulting in an increase of about 265 percent from that period's trough to its peak.

The meteoric and parabolic nature of the NASDAQ move captured the imagination of every market observer and participant. The collective wisdom of the marketplace was sending an unequivocal message—the stock market is going higher—and analysts and money managers were telling investors that their only risk was that of not being fully invested. The purveyors of that happy talk inundated the financial news programs and dispensed the type of stock picks that one would have expected to hear at cocktail parties. In many ways, the period had evolved into one of uninhibited excess, distinguished by an unbelievable level of professional irresponsibility on the part of the financial community.

The superenthusiastic rhetoric and hype were repeated so often by so many that they began to be viewed as reality, both in the financial markets and in the technology-related business community. What was developing was felt by many to be just the beginning of a long-lasting period of tech-induced prosperity.

The technology mania was built on the thesis that the Internet was such a powerful growth engine that it would drive demand for both hardware and software products for many years.

The explosive performance of IPOs created the impression that investing in these companies of the future was the opportunity of a lifetime. As
was the case in the great Ponzi scheme of 1920, the huge gains achieved by
early investors served to whet the appetites of those who unfortunately got
caught in the inevitable collapse of NASDAQ.

While Charles Ponzi obviously understood that he could not keep his
scheme going for too long, he apparently couldn't resist the temptation that
the remarkable flow of new money provided.

It should also have been obvious to Wall Street, Inc. that the stock prices
of companies that kept losing more money, quarter by quarter, year by year,
would not, and could not, be expected to keep growing exponentially. But
when everybody is getting rich, why should anybody complain about trivi-
alities such as earnings and valuations?

In my January 20, 2000, article "Rationality vs. the Market," which has
been previously referred to, I discussed a "sampling of 'story' stocks that are
priced on prospects for meaningful profits at some time in the future." Three
of the five stocks listed in Table 2.6 have gone bankrupt. At the time, Pegasus Communications was trading at $112 per share, PSI Net at $94, and Vertical Net at $252.

Amazon also has not fared too well in regard to either earnings or
stock price. It posted EPS losses of $4.02 in 2000 and $1.53 in 2001. The
article stated:

> Just recently two Internet analysts were asked to recommend a "must
> own" stock—and they both selected Amazon, even though it has experi-
> enced large and increasing losses since its inception. One week later, it
> was reported that Amazon would have to raise one billion dollars in a
> stock or convertible bond offering because it would not have enough
> money to see it through to reaching profitability.

One of the analysts in that TV interview was Mary Meeker, whose
judgment and motives in pushing so many Internet stocks have been

Table 2.6   EPS Data for Five "Story" Stocks

	1996	1997	1998	1999	1/01 Price
Amazon.com	(0.05)	(0.21)	(0.84)	(1.80)	62
Pegasus Comm.	(1.56)	(3.02)	(6.64)	(8.76)	112
PSI Net	(1.40)	(1.14)	(5.32)	(5.66)	94
Vertical Net		(0.47)	(0.64)	(0.75)	252
Yahoo!*	(0.01)	(0.07)	0.06	0.10	176

* Split-adjusted.

brought into question by several reports in business magazines. The other analyst may very well have been Henry Blodgett, but I cannot be absolutely sure of that.

Amazon's stock price responded by moving from about $65 to $85 on the strength of those and other recommendations, as analysts seemed to be falling all over each other in order to gain favor for their investment banking units in the upcoming $1 billion Amazon offering.

Another of the Internet favorites was Yahoo! For all five of the companies listed in Table 2.6, the logic of those valuations was mind-bending. At their peaks, Yahoo! was valued at about $150 billion and Amazon at about $42 billion.

As I stated in my article, the analysts had succeeded in building a mystique about the stories they were presenting based on "The idea . . . that you are paying for the promise of the future and that you must own [these stocks] at any price."

A charitable view of what happened might be that as individual and professional investors reacted to the proliferating story lines—and drove the stocks higher—the analysts began to believe more strongly in their own wisdom and invincibility, encouraging them to issue even more bolder recommendations. But there are strong indications that the analysts and the institutions that they represented had more self-serving interests that motivated their actions.

These five stocks were obviously strong "short-sale" candidates, even more so than Transitron (mentioned in Chapter 1), but with many Internet stocks having demonstrated the ability to jump 10 to 20 points in a day with the backing of Wall Street, Inc., the exercise of caution certainly seemed warranted. Obviously, the bulls were not at all burdened by any such sense of cautious restraint in their buying.

The emotionally charged atmosphere that was generated by the raging bull market caused even normally rational investors to rethink their approach. In essence, investors' expectations had been ratcheted up by stories of huge gains being achieved by more aggressive investors. In one example cited by a money manager serving individual accounts, one of his clients withdrew his money in a rage because the client's young and inexperienced son was achieving 60 percent gains compared to the money manager's 20 percent gains. The result was that intense pressure developed for all money managers to produce strong relative gains—or risk losing clients and assets.

Even some of the most successful hedge fund managers eventually succumbed to the pressure to produce by playing the technology and Internet game (against their better judgment), only to lose billions as they tried to make up for lost time by making huge bets at the wrong time.

Without doubt, the engine that drove the Internet boom can be summed up by one acronym: IPO. Everything had fallen into place, and all the financial gears had meshed perfectly—venture capitalists, investment bankers, fund managers, entrepreneurs, a compelling Internet story, and eager individual investors.

The maxim that success breeds success could not have been more applicable than it was for the IPO market. The enthusiastic response to early offerings clearly served to attract the notice of investors, thereby assuring the oversubscription of the next batch of offerings.

The underwriters did their part by emphasizing the potential of the revolutionary products that these companies had under development, even though many of the IPO candidates in question had little or no operating record. In addition, however, what helped make the offerings so successful was the fact that only 5 to 10 percent of the outstanding shares were being sold in the IPO, amounting to as few as 3 million shares in some cases, thereby creating a rather artificial supply-demand imbalance. In fact, a lawsuit was initiated against Credit Suisse First Boston concerning an illegal practice in which allocations of IPO shares to institutional clients were made contingent upon what amounted to kickbacks in the form of hugely inflated trading commissions on subsequent trading business. In essence, it had been a matter of having to "pay to play."

In their excellent book *The Internet Bubble*, published in 1999, Anthony B. Perkins and Michael C. Perkins catalogue the inner workings of the financial community pertaining to the part it played in the Internet episode, and present the perspective and detail that only professional insiders can provide. The very first page of the book succinctly sums up what was happening as follows:

> The mania surrounding Internet companies has translated into too much venture capital, too many Internet startups, and too many Internet IPOs, driving both private and public company valuations to insane levels.

The question that can be rightfully asked, then, is, if these authors could understand the lunacy of the situation and write about it in 1999, how could the financial community have succeeded in propagating its myth that there was a pot of gold at the end of the Internet rainbow?

One answer, of course, is to blame the inherent greed of the individual investors who played along in an obvious game. But lawsuits that began to surface in the post-Enron environment have alleged obviously questionable practices that tied brokerage analysts to the investment banking activities of their firms. Were analysts' strong buy ratings based on the fact that their compensation was tied to investment banking relationships and profits? The mounting evidence is quite compelling.

The harsh reality is that if an investment banking firm's analysts do not issue positive and glowing research reports about a company, the lucrative underwriting business will go to some other firm.

A reverse twist to that behavior was described in an April 16, 2002, *Wall Street Journal* article describing how a company demoted its original underwriter (Piper Jaffray) from the lead underwriting position. The retribution was swift: Piper Jaffray's analyst would no longer cover the company. One money manager was quoted as saying, "It's a dirty little secret that if you lose the banking business, the reason for covering that company disappears." And as would be expected, Piper Jaffray's spokesperson noted that coverage was dropped because of a "variety of business considerations."

Certainly there is no question but that Piper Jaffray and other firms are free to decide what companies their research group will cover. The error of commission occurs, however, when analysts issue intentionally misleading reports and recommendations in order to help the firm secure and retain investment banking relations. That is the thrust of a number of lawsuits seeking restitution of losses based upon what were deemed to be "fraudulent" recommendations.

During an April 15, 2002, CNBC discussion of the New York attorney general's lawsuit against Merrill Lynch, a previous settlement of $500,000 paid to an investor was brought up. The guest was James K. Glassman, coauthor of *Dow 36,000*. Glassman suggested that the investor could have limited his losses if he had followed Glassman's book's advice about having a diversified portfolio.

That may be excellent advice, but it wasn't responsive to the main issue. The host, Larry Kudlow, then proceeded to rail against the injustice of such awards, concluding that, while there had been "mistakes" made by analysts, "Wall Street is not a bucket shop."

Some mistakes. A few very direct questions could have quickly settled that issue. Was it a simple oversight type of mistake in which analysts failed to notice huge and growing losses in companies that they continued to tout—the very same companies that, just coincidently, were in the market for debt and secondary stock offerings?

On what basis could Pegasus Communications, PSI Net, and Vertical Net (Table 2.6) have been considered attractive "buys"? And although Amazon is still in business, could it really have qualified as a "must own" stock, as stated by Mary Meeker?

Hundreds of Internet-related companies have gone bankrupt and faded not only from the stock tables, but also from memory. A few survivors, however, are enough to portray a vivid picture of the tenor of the times during the Internet IPO craze.

Among the current survivors are former high-fliers like Ariba (Figure 2.6), a Web software and services company, and Ask Jeeves (Figure 2.7), a company with a Web site question-and-answer search format. One could conclude that their stock prices just got somewhat ahead of earnings expectations that did not materialize.

Safeguard Scientific (SFE), whose chart resembles that of Ariba and Ask Jeeves, had been a public company for many years before the Internet bubble. It had basically built a portfolio of technology companies for which it had provided start-up venture capital funding. As the IPO market heated up, some of these start-ups were brought public, creating substantial gains for SFE. The financial community then proceeded to project the value of SFE's remaining portfolio of potential IPOs, which to analysts seemed like money in the bank.

But when the wild assumptions about the "first-mover" advantage in selling just about anything on the Web disintegrated, these stocks and the IPO market fell apart. SFE, which had traded at a high of $100 per share, subsequently declined to just over $1 per share.

For a while, everybody seemed to be getting rich. And the stock tips came not only from cocktail parties, but from barbers and restaurant owners who watched CNBC and kept their computers on in back-room offices. They had been bitten by the bug—and so had their customers.

For me, one good indicator of market sentiment was the length of the line that formed at the local Fidelity office. When the market was really frothy, the lines were long even with five or more customer service people behind the counter. On one particularly busy day, an older couple in their mid to late sixties approached the counter and stated that they wanted to invest in the stock market. They were befuddled by the normal questions concerning their investment preferences and could not even complete the application without help—they just wanted to invest in the stock market. This was the surest sign that market psychology was reaching a frenzied fever pitch.

It seems that periodically one market guru or another tends to gain favor, whether it be Joe Granville, Elaine Garzarelli, or Abby Joseph Cohen. For the most part, their stardom lasts until the market selects another messenger with a more appealing vision.

FIGURE 2.6   Ariba Price Chart

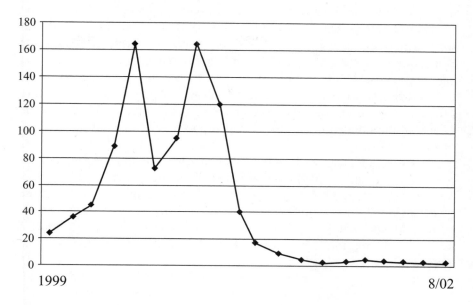

1999   8/02

FIGURE 2.7   Ask Jeeves Price Chart

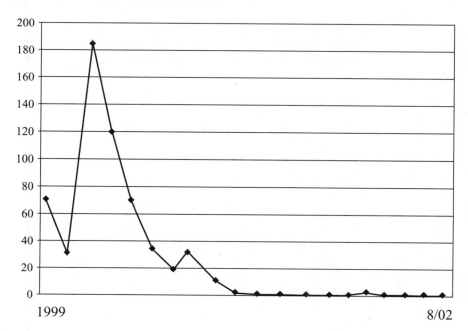

1999   8/02

Probably the most influential market mover outside of the brokerage community during the Internet bubble was George Gilder, author of "The Gilder Technology Report." In a *Boston Globe* article (March 20, 2000), that coincided almost exactly with the NASDAQ peak, he was referred to as the "Sage of the Berkshires" and a "technology futurist."

In that article, Gilder emphasized that "he is only telling readers which technologies he finds the most elegant, not which stocks are about to take off." He claimed not to "study the prices of these companies." But as the *Globe* article pointed out, his report also presented "a model portfolio of favored stocks."

His reputation grew to such a point that when companies were mentioned in his report, "[they] often see their share prices soar."

At the time, the *Globe* article noted that some of Gilder's longtime picks included JDS Uniphase (Figure 2.5), Global Crossing, and Qualcomm. At one of his technology conferences, he was asked, "Should I keep Global Crossing?" His answer was, "Sure. The company may soon be acquired."

Global Crossing has filed for bankruptcy and has been investigated for accounting irregularities, and JDS Uniphase had to write down over $50 billion of acquisition-related goodwill. Qualcomm, for its part, subsequently declined from $180 per share to $25 and was down 86 percent from its 2000 high.

Gilder seemed to want to have it both ways. He purported to convey technological developments and said, "I don't study the prices of these companies. I don't write about them because they're low or not write about a great technology because it's overvalued." However, his model portfolio conveyed a different message—the message that his subscribers were paying for.

While Gilder was ostensibly detached from Wall Street, Inc., his proven market-moving track record was not only recognized but also exploited by the financial community. In effect, Gilder's stock selections and commentary served to provide a certain stamp of approval and legitimacy for subsequent analysts' reports.

Warren Buffett, however, is a conspicuously different kind of guru. His fundamental approach (based on speech excerpts published in *Fortune*) seems to be built on a pragmatic view of the world of business. As a starting point, Buffett points out that over the long term, growth in nominal GDP will probably average only 5 percent per year, assuming a 2 percent inflation rate and a 3 percent real GDP level. On that basis, Buffett expects the overall potential growth of equity prices to be well below most investors' expectations.

His other more important point is that the return to stockholders inevitably comes from what the business earns over time, and that stockholders should consider their investments as if they were owners of the business, not just owners of stock. Following Buffett's basic tenet, how could one possibly have even contemplated valuations of $55 billion for Sycamore Networks or $150 billion for Yahoo!?

But Buffett's long-standing views about investing were totally ignored by the marketplace. What was in fact going on was described in a March 14, 2000, *New York Times* article by Thomas L. Friedman, in which he quotes a broker friend alluding to "panic buying" calls from those "asking to buy any Internet stock." That broker was troubled "because never have more people been investing in more stocks of companies about which they don't have a clue—not a clue."

Friedman also quotes a bear fund manager whose letter to shareholders referred to the fact that

> Certain tech stocks his firm had shorted—because they have no fundamentals or earnings prospects and are simply hyped by analysts and bankers—go up in price as they rack up losses . . . while the non-tech value stocks he bought . . . go down in price the more they rack up earnings.

That was a frustrating feeling experienced by many investors, myself included. In my article of January 20, 2000, I had made a similar point as follows:

> A somewhat bizarre consequence of breaking the conventional rules of valuation in order to justify infinite PEs and unlimited prices, is the logic that since PEs don't matter at all, conventional companies can be ignored no matter how low their PEs get.

In that article, I contrasted the record of the "story" stocks in Table 2.6 with a group of homebuilders (Table 2.7) that had recorded excellent earnings and were selling at P/Es in the 3 to 6 range. That comparison illustrated the vast divide that had come to separate the "new economy" from the "old economy."

Table 2.7   EPS and P/E Data for Selected Homebuilders*

	1995	1996	1997	1998	1999	CIGR	P/E
D. R. Horton	0.74	0.87	1.15	1.56	2.49	35%	4.7
MDC Holdings	0.86	0.98	1.18	2.32	3.95	46%	3.8
M/I Schottenstein	1.12	1.60	2.15	3.26	4.65	43%	3.0
Toll Brothers	1.47	1.50	1.86	2.25	2.71	17%	6.6

* EPS data prior to stock splits.

Again, I could not bring myself to risk shorting these obviously insanely valued high-flying new-economy stocks, but I concluded that the home-building stocks were being indiscriminately sold, thereby providing an out-standing buying opportunity.

In April 1999 I purchased shares of M/I Schottenstein Homes (Figure 2.8), a NYSE stock that was selling at a P/E of about 5. To my total amaze-ment, the stock trended downward as NASDAQ was soaring. Indications were that some institutional holders were unloading, especially during the November 1999–February 2000 period, obviously using MHO as a source of funds with which to buy more new-economy stocks.

Since the stock was selling well below book value, the company initi-ated a stock repurchase program to take advantage of the breakdown in the theoretical efficiency of the stock market.

For my part, since there was no conclusive way to judge where the bot-tom might be, I established a plan to buy at particular price levels on the way down. For 1999, MHO's EPS increased by 43.5 percent and amounted to a postsplit value of $2.34. My last purchase was at the February 2000 postsplit low of $6.375 per share—which had MHO valued at a P/E of 2.7. That last purchase was just pure luck, since it was part of the plan to buy at every half-point decline (in the presplit stock).

FIGURE 2.8   M/I Schottenstein Price Chart

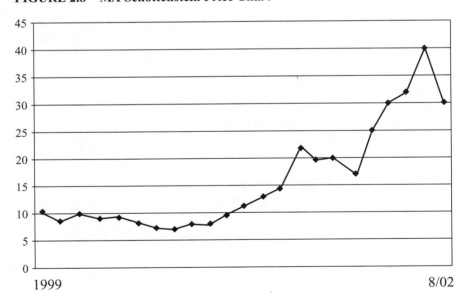

1999   8/02

By any rational analytical measure, it would seem inconceivable that analysts could not bring themselves to give these stocks at least a passing glance. But during that period, MHO was able to attract only minimal analyst interest in the brokerage community—there were no underwritings in the offing, so there was little incentive for firms to follow the company. Increasing confidence in the industry's prospects prompted me to also take a position in Meritage Corp. in February 2000.

Comparing the charts of the Internet stocks and the homebuilding stocks clearly reveals the dramatic impact that the Internet craze had on investment decisions at the time. Up until March 2000, it had been Internet all the way, and fund managers had been dumping the likes of homebuilding stocks at throw-away prices. The plain fact of the matter was that fund managers had chosen to roll the dice—along with all the other speculators. After all, it wasn't their own money that they were playing with.

It often seems that the overwhelming power in the hands of Wall Street, Inc. serves to force individual investors to playing its game. The home-building stock example is an instance where sticking to fundamentals, even if it takes going against the grain, can work by taking advantage of opportunities created by the Street's misjudgments and follies.

While the boom lasted, it seemed that a lot of people were benefiting from the roaring stock market. The stories of instant IPO multimillionaires and billionaires provided further evidence of the magical quality of the new economy.

One rather interesting and telling anecdote appeared in the October 8, 2001, annual *Forbes* 400 issue. After a very successful IPO offering, the stock held by the CEO of an Internet company was suddenly worth over $200 million. The following paragraph, titled "Filly Folly," is apropos of the time:

Michael Donahue plunged into Wellington's [Florida] polo life with the kind of abandon you'd expect from a young Internet executive. The 39-year-old head of Interworld, a small Internet software company, began building a cavernous 56-stall barn in Wellington soon after his company's public offering in August, 1999. Donahue persuaded Salomon Smith Barney to lend him $14 million to help finance the structure against his 4.3 million shares of Interworld, at the time worth $200 million. Alas, the stock dropped out of the intergalactic range. Even after a 1-for-50 reverse split, the shares go for only 85 cents apiece, making Donahue's stake worth all of $473,000. A third party assumed the loan, took the deed to the barn and put it on the market for $8 million. So far, no takers.

This was more than just "filly folly"—the story is another metaphor for the folly of Wall Street, Inc. Can one imagine an investment banking firm with the long and distinguished heritage of Salomon Smith Barney taking a company like that public in the first place, then further suspending judgment by actually believing that the stock represented good and sufficient collateral for a $14 million loan?

For those who dream of riches, the *Forbes* 400 issue gives one a chance to hope—the price of admission for the 2001 listing had dropped to a mere $600 million.

The Millennium Party Ends

The new millennium was being ushered in following an especially enthusiastic stock market surge that closed out the fourth quarter of 1999. One could not have written a more perfect script—just at the time that the Internet craze was at its peak, the end-of-the-century Y2K "problem" prompted the Federal Reserve to dramatically increase the money supply.

Simply put, the looming Y2K problem was based on the fact that the data stored in computers had initially used only two digits to designate the year (like 10 for 1910) because of the limited memory capacity in early computers. At the turn of the century, then, computers would not be able to distinguish between 1910 and 2010—which could understandably present a problem. Technological improvements had overcome this memory limitation long ago, but a significant number of both corporate and government computers were deemed not to be Y2K "compliant."

The concern was that the information from these noncompliant computers could contaminate the nation's entire computer network and create widespread disruptions throughout the banking, power plant, water utility, and air-traffic control systems.

Senate hearings on Y2K preparedness served to further heighten the anxiety, resulting in warnings that urged individuals to be prepared for these eventualities by increasing their cash on hand, and to stock up on food, water, batteries, and so on.

Corporations spent many hundreds of billions of dollars to replace many of their hardware and software systems, in many cases earlier than necessary, rather than go to the expense of just trying to deal with a Y2K "fix." This upgrade cycle, however, had the obvious effect of borrowing from future computer capital spending.

As many had actually predicted, there wasn't even a Y2K ripple. But for the stock market, the Y2K event had added to an already very significant speculative Internet wave. All that extra capital spending in the years leading up to the millennium had given the stock market a tremendous boost, and with the Federal Reserve pumping an estimated $80 billion into the system during the last quarter of 1999, the wave got even bigger.

There can be no question that the Federal Reserve badly misjudged the situation, thereby exaggerating the final stock market speculative surge. The Federal Reserve is the lender of last resort, and it certainly would have been able to respond immediately to any Y2K-related problems as they arose. It also no doubt misjudged the actions of investors, who took advantage of the excess liquidity to borrow on margin in order to buy more stocks.

A January 1, 2001, *Red Herring* article by Arnold Berman of Wit Soundview discusses the elements of the spending bubble as illustrated in Figure 2.9. While the figure does not quantify actual spending levels, it conveys a reasonably accurate indication of the contributions to information technology (IT) spending starting in 1997.

The figure clearly depicts the combined impact from

1.   Global Y2K emergency spending
2.   Upstart communications service spending
3.   Dot.com spending
4.   Global Web spending

FIGURE 2.9   Information Technology Spending Patterns

POP GOES THE SPENDING BUBBLE

Several factors pushed IT budgets to unsustainable highs over the last few years.

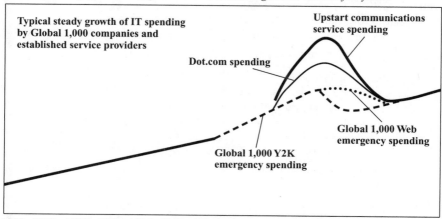

1990 1991 1992 1993 1994 1995 1996 1997 1998 1999 2000 2001 2002 2003
Source: Wit Soundview.

The article elaborates as follows:

> The mania period was grounded in the presumption that technology
> spending would accelerate for ages. With the benefit of hindsight, we can
> see that the spending spree was a temporary phenomenon. By late 1999
> and in the first quarter 2000, legions of technology companies were gen-
> erating revenues that defied the law of large numbers. But then, in the
> second quarter of 2000, pockets of fundamental weakness began to
> emerge. All phone sales disconnected. Back-end chip equipment makers
> disappointed. PC demand was slack. And the fundamentals of e-com-
> merce began to erode. Throughout the remainder of 2000 and into
> 2001 . . . those pockets of weakness have deepened and multiplied.

The millennium punch bowl had, indeed, been taken away—much to the
dismay of shocked and disbelieving investors. Just as everything had
seemed to go right during the boom times, a host of unfavorable developments were now conspiring to increase the severity of the unfolding technology downturn.

What had gone wrong, however, cannot be ascribed in any way to any
failure of the technology itself—it had done an impressive job in developing
all the complex hardware and software necessary to make the Internet a reality. Rather, it was the financial community under the Wall Street, Inc.
umbrella that recognized the opportunity of a lifetime and rode it for all it
was worth. When the prospects for unimaginable profits began to be vali-
dated by early IPO successes, the financial community went into overdrive.

A July 14, 2000, *Wall Street Journal* article tells of a company's executive having "15 different investment banks courting him with regular phone
calls. The pitch . . . was you've got $2 million in sales, go for it." He did go
for it, with Goldman Sachs as its lead underwriter.

One of the most revealing discussions reported by the *Wall Street
Journal* article involved one particular interview as follows:

> Goldman officials deny that their standards slipped, and contend that the
> firm . . . passed on deals that rivals chose to underwrite. Mr. Koenig adds
> that criticism of underwriters is off-target. If an Internet start-up with
> losses exceeding revenue goes public and goes to a $2.2 billion valuation,
> whose fault is that? It's a tough philosophical argument . . . is it an under-
> writer's responsibility to determine whether the market is overvalued or
> undervalued? Investment bankers wouldn't be making a good living if
> that was required.

There need be no worry about the Goldman Sachs partners making a
good living, especially after their own IPO, which netted them tens of millions of dollars each.

And there need be no worry about the venture capital firms that pro-vided start-up financing for many of these IPOs and received stock for which they paid pennies per share. According to one former venture capital-ist quoted by the *Wall Street Journal*, "You could invest in a company, take it public and cash out before you proved your business model." In addition, analysts like Mary Meeker and Henry Blodgett got their share for stoking the fires of the boiler room.

Then there are all those mutual funds that invest the money entrusted to them by individuals. What about their investment due diligence? The *Wall Street Journal* article relates an example known to have been a standard practice in the IPO market. In this instance, a mutual fund manager got an extra allotment of Ariba stock (Figure 2.6) when he agreed to buy a certain amount of stock in the aftermarket. The intent was quite obvious: Any addi-tional buying pressure would further unbalance the already limited supply and high demand situation, in this instance helping to move Ariba from its $23 per share offering price up to more than $90 on the first day (prior to two 2:1 stock splits). Thanks to such arrangements, that fund achieved a 249 percent gain in 1999. In 2002, ARBA was trading below $3 per share on a postsplit basis.

In another example, the *Wall Street Journal* article describes how one typical fund manager approached the question of investing in Internet stocks:

> To catch the Web wave—and keep up with peers' performance—many fund managers loaded up on Internet stocks even though many in their hearts believed the shares to be overvalued. Twice last year, Mr. Tracey, until recently manager of Oppenheimer Enterprise Fund, thought a mam-moth correction was coming and sold many Internet stocks. Both times he was wrong. So, after the second time, he jumped at the chance a few weeks later to buy into the IPO of an industrial auctioneer called FreeMarkets Inc. [Figure 2.10]. It was valued at $1.8 billion based on its IPO price, despite 12-month sales of just $16 million and steep losses. But Mr. Tracey figured that similar companies were trading at far richer levels, and as to whether those valuations were ridiculous: "I said I'm going to suspend judgment for the moment."

That proved profitable for Tracey, who watched FreeMarkets rocket from its IPO price of $48 in December 1999 to $280 the first day of trading. He held on as it roared to $370 in January, then dumped it in February at $215. That strategy helped Tracey's fund post a 105 percent return.

How could all of these participants have been expected to resist the obvious temptation? It was like a youngster finding him- or herself in a

FIGURE 2.10   FreeMarkets Price Chart

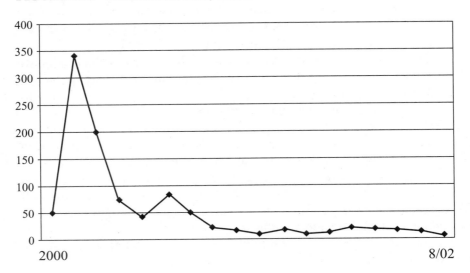

candy store with no proprietor and no adult supervision. As stated previously, the excesses were there for all to see, and so it was all the more galling to many to be accused of "not getting it" by the very same participants who were benefiting the most from the game of make-believe.

In that regard, one question cries out for an answer: How could the CEOs of the investment banking and brokerage firms have allowed those incredible recommendations and price objectives to be issued under the firm's name? Was there no pride, no quality control, no thought or concern about the firm's reputation? All that apparently seemed to matter was the concern about "making a good living," as Koenig of Goldman Sachs implied in his comments.

The IPO market was reminiscent of a classic gold rush, but this time the prospectors didn't use picks and shovels. The advice to "strike while the iron is hot" was well heeded, and every potential IPO deal was expedited and put on a fast track to meet the seemingly insatiable demand.

However, the financial community understood full well that there was one big risk—an Achilles' heel—that could unhinge everything. The whole IPO game was predicated on these start-ups being able to continue to raise additional money to fund their spending—and their losses. Of course, that would also happily provide the financial community with a continuous flow of underwriting fees.

In fact, the venture capitalists and investment bankers who served on the boards of these companies as advisers encouraged them to spend their cash as quickly as possible in order to gain as strong a competitive advantage as possible.

Many companies, like Global Crossing, Exodus, Covad, and scores of others, did, in fact, succeed in raising huge amounts of money in the debt market to meet their aggressive expansion plans. But their high cash-burn rates required more and more trips to the capital markets.

For a while, the increasingly horrendous losses were interpreted as a good sign—namely, that these companies were planting the seeds of long-term profitability. But a funny thing happened on the way to nirvana: The money spigot began to close because of a growing concern that many of these companies might not be able to service their increasing debt burdens. With their ability to borrow more money greatly reduced, the handwriting was on the wall.

Many of the venture capital funds soon began to feel the pressure. With conventional borrowing sources drying up, these funds had to go back to their wealthy investors and pension funds to request additional follow-on contributions to support the various developmental companies in the funds' portfolio. With greatly diminished prospects for IPO gains, investors were more inclined to cash out than to contribute more.

The Internet happy talk had helped fuel the mania on the upside; now the computation of how long these companies could survive without new financing began to contribute to a developing aura of gloom. The IPO gold rush days were over.

The 2001 Earnings Collapse

The dimensions of the 2001 earnings collapse experienced by companies in the technology sector can be measured by the earnings results of the 22 high-profile companies listed in Table 2.2.

Prior to the meltdown, large companies like Intel, Microsoft, Cisco, and Dell not only were ringing up impressive percentage gains in operating income, but also were augmenting those results on the side with gains from venture capital investments.

The tenor of the times was captured by a February 8, 2002, *Wall Street Journal* article entitled "Intel Rolls Dice on Tech Upstarts—and Hits Jackpot." Apparently, Intel had invested $1.2 billion in 1999 alone in about 250 start-ups—mostly Internet-related companies—and at the end of 1999 its portfolio was valued at $8.2 billion. In the fourth quarter of 1999, it reported a $327 million investment income gain, and it had almost $6 billion in unrealized gains.

Some of Intel's "blockbuster gains" came from investments in CMGI, Red Hat Software, Broadcom, Inktomi, Covad Communications, eToys, and iVillage.

Mr. Leslie Vadasz, head of corporate investments at Intel, must have been quite adept at getting in and out of these investments, because the latter three companies went bankrupt, and the others have declined precipitously from their highs.

In 2001, not only were Intel's operating results weak, but there were no "blockbuster gains" to help the bottom line.

Another interesting foray into the world of Internet investing concerns the legendary George Soros. A May 22, 2000, *Wall Street Journal* story chronicles the decision-making process that prompted Soros to shift away from his belief that "the Internet craze would end badly." Although Soros felt "nervous" about the tech sector, his Quantum hedge fund had been performing poorly, and it needed a boost. His chief fund manager, Stanley Druckenmiller, hired a money manager who "didn't mind paying sky-high prices for tech stocks."

In a defining moment, Druckenmiller heard Intel chairman Andrew Grove speak at the Allen & Co. annual Sun Valley, Idaho, conference of corporate executives. He became so convinced about the new economy that he loaded up on these stocks and sold some old-economy stocks short, helping the Quantum fund gain 35 percent in 1999.

When NASDAQ began to crumble in March 2000, Soros began to worry. One investment in particular proved to be contentious. The Soros Quantum fund had bought VeriSign (Figure 2.11), a network security services company, at $50 per share. After a visit by VeriSign's CEO, Quantum bought more at $258, doubling its investment to $600 million in early March. When the stock dropped to $135 in early April, Soros reportedly said, "VeriSign is going to kill us. We should take our exposure down." Druckenmiller resisted, saying, "This is different than other Internet plays." As the market continued to go against Quantum, Druckenmiller resigned, later stating that "I overplayed my hand."

VeriSign reported a loss of $3.1 billion in 2000 and a much larger loss of $13.3 billion in 2001—profits were collapsing in the whole technology sector.

Cisco had achieved such a commanding presence as both a technology leader and a stock market favorite that its peak P/E soared to 225 in early

FIGURE 2.11 **Verisign Price Chart**

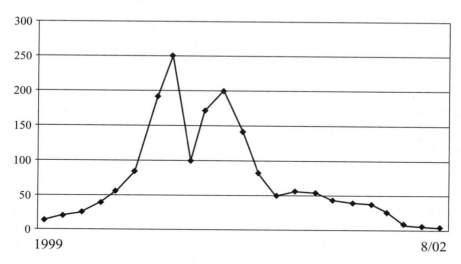

2000, and it briefly attained a market value of approximately $600 billion. During the late 1990s it had capitalized on its stock's high value by making dozens of acquisitions in an attempt to further solidify and expand its market reach. In many instances, acquisitions were pursued with dual objectives in mind: expanding Cisco's own product line and at the same time swallowing up a potential competitor.

While Cisco's high-priced and highly prized stock clearly would have been expected to provide it with a significant advantage in negotiating with any company of its choosing, it apparently was in such a rush to announce some of these deals that, in one case, it traded stock valued at about $7 billion for an unproven and unprofitable company that was in the early stages of developing a line of advanced product offerings.

In many instances, however, the announcement of a sizable acquisition was deemed to represent a coup for Cisco and would result in an increase in its market value by more than the purchase price. Nevertheless, one has to wonder what Wall Street would have thought about Cisco's acquisition spree if the deals had been paid for using cash rather than stock.

In its fiscal year ended July 2001, Cisco reported a $1 billion loss versus the year earlier's peak profit of $2.67 billion. For the 5 years ending in July 2001, Cisco had earned a total of $6.2 billion, or $0.85 per share. From that perspective, one has to question the degree to which Cisco exercised good judgment in paying more than its total 5-year earnings for a single unproven start-up—even given the fact that it had used highly inflated stock in that transaction.

The dot.com companies, as a group, had never achieved profitability. But their profligate spending patterns, using the money raised from their IPOs, had prompted other companies in the Internet-related sectors to expand quickly in the race to capture their own share of that spending.

The new buzzwords like B2C (business-to-consumer) and B2B (business-to-business) sounded like music to the ears of dazzled investors. New companies sprang up overnight, including online advertising companies like Doubleclick and Web site designers like Sapient and Razorfish. These stocks soared on the high promise of the Internet's future—but crashed with a vengeance when that promise went unmet.

Companies like Exodus that provided Web-hosting services expanded much too aggressively. Exodus built costly centers that promised the dot.com companies a full-service capability that would provide them with a secure and efficient means of filling all their future online needs. As Exodus and hundreds of dot.com companies filed for bankruptcy, the demand for computer servers, memory devices, and similar infrastructure products took a big hit.

But the biggest hit in terms of collapsing demand came from the telecom sector. The assumption had been that in order for the vision of a totally online world to become a reality, the telecom companies would need to expand their capacity in order to move an ever-increasing stream of data at faster and faster transmission speeds to serve both business and residential end users.

As previously discussed, the CLECS and the incumbent carriers were competing for the DSL (digital subscriber line) broadband business, and both were racing against the challenge of high-speed cable modem services being offered by the cable companies. Since it appeared to many that DSL had a natural advantage because it utilized existing phone lines, a flood of new entrants were attracted to the DSL equipment market. However, the fundamental conflict between the Baby Bells, who owned the phone lines, and the Internet service providers (ISPs) who wanted to use them degenerated into a confrontation that centered on the alleged noncompetitive and monopolistic practices of the regional Bell operating companies (RBOCs). In the end, the pricing power of the RBOCs essentially squeezed out the ISP competition, and DSL providers like North Point Communications, Flashcom, PSI Net, Winstar, and Covad all went bankrupt.

The demise of so many ISPs in the DSL debacle had a telling impact on revenues for companies like Cisco and Nortel. Without the pressure from the ISPs, the RBOCs began to take their time in assessing their future DSL strategy—especially at a time when weak earnings and high debt levels were forcing cutbacks in capital expenditures.

There are also two very revealing telecom cases involving Winstar and Global Crossing in which a number of the "smart money" crowd became enmeshed.

In both cases, the logic and desirability of building worldwide fiber-optic data transmission systems certainly couldn't have been faulted from a long-term or a conceptual point of view. However, how could start-up companies like these hope to implement such an incredibly ambitious and impressively grandiose objective? The answer is that they got started by convincing other like-minded enthusiasts to either help them raise or directly lend them the seed money.

In the case of Winstar, its management was able to bring Microsoft on board as a major investor, and then succeeded in negotiating structured finance programs with companies like Cisco, Compaq, and Lucent for the purchase of equipment.

One of Winstar's financing deals had raised over $1 billion from the issuance of convertible preferred stock from a number of investors, including Credit Suisse First Boston (CSFB). Wall Street, Inc. got another piece of the action by underwriting a $1.6 billion Winstar debt offering that netted Salomon Smith Barney and CSFB a hefty $50 million commission.

The fact that Winstar reported a $1 billion loss in early 2001 should not have come as a great surprise. But Jack Grubman, Salomon's analyst, reacted by reiterating his view that the stock was "severely undervalued." CSFB's analyst also remained extremely bullish about Winstar's prospects. It should not be surprising that both these analysts were employed by Winstar's lead investment bankers.

When Winstar delayed the release of its SEC 10-K filing in April 2001, all hope that it could continue to borrow more money to keep its vision alive vanished.

Among those left with huge losses in the Winstar episode were the equipment suppliers. These were technology companies, not bankers. No matter how anxious the suppliers might have been to close a sale, did they not stop to consider why Winstar would feel the need to turn to them for financing help? Could the reason possibly be that Winstar was so financially overextended that the banks and the capital markets were having second thoughts about Winstar's debt level?

Global Crossing's story is very similar. Its massive undertaking in building a system of fiber-optic cable lines connecting 200 cities in 27 countries in the Americas, Europe, and Asia required it to go heavily into debt. It was among the numerous telecom recipients of a combined $320 billion in loans from investment bankers and banks. As a result, money-losing Global Crossing was burdened with $600 million in annual interest costs on $7.5 billion of debt, along with $200 million in preferred dividends.

Apparently, a well-known name, a high-profile image, and a high market capitalization were sufficient collateral for the banks that lent these companies billions. Of course, the handsome fees involved might have been another consideration.

It is hard to comprehend the fact that such a massive suspension of judgment affected so many. It is almost as if a driver were going 100 mph through the center of town, going through stop signs and red lights, without eliciting even a shrug from the entire police force witnessing it. However, since everything seemed to be going so well for so many during the good times, cynics were hardly welcomed.

But hype alone was not enough to mask the continuing losses and huge capital spending needs of telecom companies like Global Crossing and Winstar. When the capital markets and the bankers finally decided that enough was enough, it was all over for the telecom upstarts.

As a consequence, the technology-related companies experienced the flip side of the capital spending boom, with revenues declining more than 50 percent in many cases. And if all of that wasn't enough, intimations and investigations of an alleged widespread practice of "cooking the books" would result in a further erosion of confidence. Not only did this bring the judgment and motives of many into question, but it tarnished the reputation and damaged the credibility of many others.

Whose Books Were Cooked?

"Cooking the books" is an odd expression, but everybody knows what it means. The analogy that comes to mind is that you can't always be sure about what went into the stew—which is the main idea of cooking the books, accounting-wise.

Many corporations have consistently bent the conventional rules of accounting to some extent for obvious reasons. There is always pressure on managers of publicly listed companies to meet or beat financial goals and Wall Street's expectations.

When a company consistently beats analysts' EPS projections by a single penny or two, quarter after quarter, the Street marvels at the extraordinary skill of management. Part of that game, of course, is that management "guides" analysts' projections in the first place—and, knowing the rules of the road, or more precisely the rules of the Street, that guidance is established to allow for a "positive surprise."

The other part of the equation, however, arises when, for example, end-of-quarter shipments come in lower than expected. That type of situation reflects the realities of the business world, which do not always conform to a particular master plan. But with the help of creative accounting, that, too, can be dealt with by deciding what items get included, excluded, deferred, or what have you. This may be considered to be playing with the numbers, but achieving the desired results was the primary objective to begin with.

However, when the Enron scandal broke, its impact was so devastating and far-reaching that questions concerning accounting practices finally began to surface.

What went on at Enron involved more than playing with the numbers. Even the terms *aggressive accounting* and *accounting irregularities* do not adequately reflect the serious breaches of ethics and loss of integrity at Enron.

The top management trio at Enron consisted of Chairman Kenneth Lay, CEO Jeffrey Skilling, and CFO Andrew Fastow. In an attempt to create an energy-trading giant that "would open markets across the globe in the face of entrenched, lumbering monopolies" (as noted in a February 11, 2002, *Business Week* article), Enron had to find innovative ways to fund the implementation of its plan, the scope of which was implied when Skilling "once compared ExxonMobil Corp. to a floundering seven-mast clipper ship."

The funding vehicles that were devised by the Skilling-Fastow team were based on special-purpose entities (SPEs) and other "increasingly complex and unusual off-balance-sheet financing that fueled Enron's growth." The revelation that CFO Fastow personally benefited from these partnerships, one of which paid Fastow a fee purported to be in the $30 million range, raised the obvious issue of conflict of interest.

But was it just Fastow and Skilling who were complicit in these immensely complicated and questionable transactions? Could they have conceived and executed all of those schemes without the active participation and cooperation of an army of investment bankers, accounting consultants, and lawyers? Does the fact that this support group was being well paid to assist clients like Enron in every creative way possible excuse the part that they played in that sorry episode?

As a consequence of the furor aroused by the Enron accounting scandal, attention began to be focused on a range of practices that could be characterized as being misleading, deceptive, and even potentially fraudulent.

For example, a number of telecom start-ups, including Global Crossing, were known to have been engaged in end-of-quarter asset swaps in which the asset sale was recorded as revenue in the income statement, while the offsetting asset purchase was treated as a balance sheet capital expenditure item. These have been deemed to be sham transactions with little or no economic value—their sole purpose was to inflate reported revenues.

In a December 24, 2001, *Fortune* article, it was reported that "lease payments from rivals will account for about $1.6 billion of Global Crossing's revenues. When asked how Global Crossing used capacity it bought from rivals—at a cost of about $1.3 billion," the CEO responded that he didn't "know the specifics of deals completed before he arrived." This was much like Enron CEO Jeffrey Skilling's congressional testimony, in which he professed to know precious little about the details of deals made by his CFO.

As previously mentioned, it has been an open secret that many companies go to great lengths to "manage" their quarterly earnings results. In fact, as the March 19, 2001, *Fortune* article "Accounting in Wonderland" relates, GE's "stunning run of profit growth—101 straight quarters—is somehow artificial, the result of managed earnings." The article points out that there is nothing illegal about that practice, but that "GE, for one, denies that it engages in such artful accounting."

The article delves into many accounting transactions in which "nothing was simple, and no one—not even the number crunchers at GE—seemed to know the difference between reality and fantasy."

When the author called GE to inform them that he "was doing a story on how confusing its financial filings are, the company informed (him) that it had won all sorts of awards for transparency."

My own attempt at unraveling the mysteries of GE's financial performance dated back to early 1999, when I requested a GE investor relations package. Included in the package were the following reprints:

1. "How Jack Welch Runs GE" (*BusinessWeek*, June 8, 1998)

2. "Builders & Titans" (*Time*, December 7, 1998)

3. "The World's Most Admired Companies" (*Fortune*, October 26, 1998)

4. "A Jack Welch Executive Speech—A Company to Be Proud Of"

5. "America's Most Admired Companies" (*Fortune*, March 1, 1999)

These reprints were certainly great promotional pieces. However, what had originally motivated my request for the package was a desire to determine how GE presented the income gains that were generated from its overfunded pension plan.

To my surprise, there was no line entry in the income statement that identified any such item. Searching further, I found the information tucked into footnote 5, which indicated that in 1998, GE had had $1.016 billion in pension income gains. This was not an inconsequential number, since GE's total reported income for the year had been $9.3 billion. No wonder GE did not want to call attention to that particular item. The question that arises, however, concerns the willingness of the analyst community and the large mutual fund investors to go along with this clever tactic. In all the appearances of analysts on GE's CNBC financial news unit, in which they universally praised GE even at P/Es that approached 50, none ever raised that issue until after the increased focus on corporate accounting practices.

In "Rationality vs. the Market," I noted that, at the time, just 15 companies had a combined market capitalization of $3.5 trillion out of an estimated $15 trillion market capitalization for all stocks. At that rate, that "would theoretically imply a total stock market universe of only 65 similarly valued companies."

My article continued:

> The huge money flows that must be put to work on a continuous basis almost forces [the managers] into high capitalization and therefore more liquid stocks. One has to wonder, therefore, whether fund managers invest based on purely objective analysis, or whether they just find ways to justify going with the big names.
>
> GE is a case in point. It has been regarded as a bellwether because of a record of consistent earnings gains. Its EPS record . . . is steady but not remarkable for a stock valued at a P/E of 45 and about 3.5 times its compound income growth rate (CIGR). Add to that the fact that in 1998 it considerably enhanced earnings by transferring approximately $1 billion from an over-funded pension plan into its income stream, and that it has a . . . tangible book value of about $1.85, it would seem hard to justify more than an average multiple for its stock [which was trading at a post-split price of $48.50 per share at the time].

Figure 2.12, which appeared in an April 29, 2002, *BusinessWeek* article, clearly depicts the extent to which GE's performance was helped by the yearly increase in its pension income. It is important to note that none of that pension income can be withdrawn from the pension fund for general corporate use—it merely represents an accounting entry based on the way overfunded pension income is treated. However, if a stock market decline were to result in an underfunded pension fund, the corporation would be required to make up the difference by contributing real dollars to the fund.

FIGURE 2.12   5-Year Earnings and Pension Income for GE

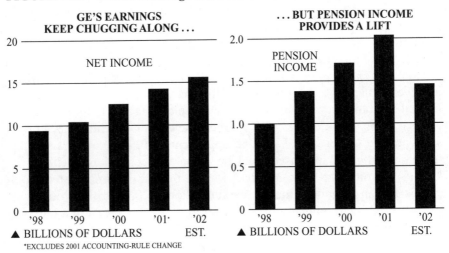

Source: General Electric Co., Standard & Poor's Equities

In addition to the contribution to absolute earnings, the inclusion of pension fund income in GE's reported results served to (1) smooth out the reported annual income gains and (2) increase the company's 5-year compound income growth rate from 11 percent to 13.4 percent.

For the investment community, having absolute earnings levels that were approximately 11 percent higher each year certainly helped to justify GE's above-average P/E multiple during that period. It should be emphasized that GE followed the existing accounting rules in the treatment of its overfunded pension plan—it just didn't go out of its way to have such a material item explicitly appear in its income statement.

And as the "Accounting in Wonderland" article pointed out, there was certainly a noticeable lack of transparency in GE's financial reports. But GE's new CEO, Jeffrey Immelt, promised that the company's annual report might well become as thick as the New York City telephone directory in its effort to provide greater disclosure.

In an interesting development, S&P has decided not to include pension income in the total earnings of the S&P 500 companies—which will have an obvious impact on the S&P 500 P/E level. That decision helps to resolve what had become an easily manipulated situation, one that helped CFOs post pension income gains in a given year that in reality were just plain fiction.

Accounting rules have basically allowed corporations to establish an expected investment rate of return for their pension fund at the beginning of each year. In so doing, management has the ability to predetermine a certain segment of its corporate income—regardless of the fund's actual investment performance. Many pension funds suffered significant declines in 2001, but it was the projected pension income, not the loss, that found its way to the income statement's bottom line.

This contradiction has been generally explained away by noting that the returns tend to average out over the long term. But since the pension income is not available to the company for corporate use in the base case, there is no reason to consider it as income—as S&P has properly concluded.

As John Bogle stated, everybody wants stock prices to go up, and company CEOs and CFOs know that in order to satisfy the Wall Street crowd, they have to actually beat expectations. This is a challenge that is not taken lightly. So, when the numbers don't add up, there are only two choices—and management gets paid big salaries to make the right choice.

In an April 14, 2001, *BusinessWeek* article entitled "The Numbers Game," one portfolio manager's comment made it clear what that choice would be:

> They, as in the past, tortured accounting to produce income statements that would be applauded by Wall Street.

A number of accounting stratagems have been available to choose from when some juggling of the numbers is called for, including the following:

1. *Pro forma accounting*, or what has been called "everything but the bad stuff." Amazon elevated this game to an art form when, for example, it reported a "pro forma operating" loss of $49 million and a "pro forma net" loss of $76 million, only to have investors later discover that Amazon actually had a net loss of $234 million.

   Similarly, giant telecom carrier Qwest Communications reported $2 billion in quarterly earnings before interest, taxes, depreciation, and amortization, or EBITDA. Shareholders had to wait weeks to find out, in a footnote to the annual results, that Qwest actually lost $116 million according to GAAP rules.

2. *Vendor financing*. If potential customers cannot purchase equipment because of credit limitations, why not have the supplier provide the financing?

   Motorola, Cisco, Lucent, and Nortel used this strategy to close deals. It was reported that Motorola was owed $1.7 billion by a Turkish wireless carrier—which it has subsequently written off.

3.   *Booking very optimistic assumptions made for pension fund income.*

4.   *Recording sales early or costs late.*

5.   *Changing assumptions that will reduce reported expenses.*

6.   *Acquiring companies, having them take big write-offs prior to the closing date, and then reversing those charges upon completion of the acquisition*—a favorite tactic attributed to Tyco International.

One additional subtle example with a slight twist involved IBM's sale of one of its units that resulted in a $300 million gain. Not only did IBM not disclose this as an extraordinary item, but it lumped the gain into its sales, general, and administrative (SG&A) expense category. Of course, the one-time gain reduced the SG&A total, making it appear that IBM's expense ratios were declining. IBM's rationale for not even reporting the sale was that it was too small to be material.

If it is difficult for even the professionals to dissect and understand the complicated financial statements of so many companies, what is an individual investor to do? A good rule that should be considered is, If you don't understand it, don't own it.

But, in getting to better deal with financial statements, it may be well to analyze the income and balance sheet statements of companies that appear to be relatively straightforward—namely, those that seem to add up in an understandable way, as is illustrated in the Gorman-Rupp example in Chapter 4.

Part Two

THE REAL DEAL: REEVALUATING INVESTMENT PRINCIPLES AND GUIDELINES

3

THE INVESTMENT FUNDAMENTALS

An Investment Perspective

The experience of the late 1990s demonstrates the degree to which investors can be influenced by overall stock market psychology, which is often based on either the latest fad or some vague prospect of ultimately huge financial gains. Given the reality of the market as it now exists, then, the critical task for the investor is to find a way to cope by establishing a plan of action that is based on a thorough review of fundamental investment principles and guidelines. Obviously, a well-grounded approach to investing must be flexible, but alternatively, a solid frame of reference may well serve to protect against the often risky temptations that are bound to present themselves.

Just for a moment, try to imagine a stock market environment without the TV financial news programs like CNBC—no analysts, money managers, or CEOs to watch or listen to as they are given the opportunity to spin their side of the story on particular stocks.

Basically, investors would be back to reading about the latest financial developments in the *Wall Street Journal, Investors Business Daily, BusinessWeek,* and other such publications. But one of the most significant pieces of news by far for the investor would come at the end of each quarter, when earnings results are reported. You really wouldn't need instant analysis to help you determine whether the results were positive or not—and if a company lost money, you wouldn't necessarily jump for joy because that loss was a few pennies less than the amount some unknown analyst had projected.

But those days are gone forever. In my article "Rationality vs. the Market," I had noted that

> The conventional wisdom is that the market is always right—that by definition market action reflects the considered and collective judgment of well-informed rational investors. If being well-informed is equated to having ready access to on-line real time information, then today's investors certainly have gained a distinct advantage in recent years.
>
> But the very technology that has created this information revolution, may have perversely disturbed and damaged the investment decision-making process.

The point of that last comment is that investing should involve more than watching CNBC for the minute-by-minute moves of stocks and the stock market. It is in this sense that some investors may have had their attention diverted from a more substantive approach to investment decision making.

In this regard, one of the most coherently expressed approaches to "objective and comparative investment analysis" was discussed in an interview with John Winthrop Wright of Wright Investors' Service in a July 6, 1981, *Forbes* article.

At the time, Wright Investors' Service was managing $1 billion of mostly pension fund money. Wright, who had previously been a businessman, described his transition to being a successful money manager:

> In 1960, not long after I sold a couple of manufacturing businesses, I realized that if I let brokerage houses invest my money, I'd soon have very little left.

The article goes on to further describe Wright's motivations:

> This was in the first great flush of the growth-stock mania and Ben Graham–type fundamental analysis was out of style. That bothered Wright. He didn't want his money managed with scant attention to the business and accounting fundamentals— things he understood.

Back in 1981, Wright's staff used computers to "evaluate 32 characteristics for each stock, many over a ten-year time-weighted period. . . . Wright's computers give every stock a complicated (but very comprehensible) rating such as AAA20."

The first letter measured investment marketability and acceptance determined by such things as how widely shares are distributed and whether or not the float is adequate.

The second letter was an indication of financial strength, arrived at by assessing debt-equity ratios, working capital and other criteria.

The third letter described profitability in terms of the rate of return on stockholders investment and how stable it has been.

The final numbers, ranging from 0 to 20, stood for growth in earnings, dividends and equity capital.

The article notes that "stocks must get at least a BBB6 rating to be eligible for Wright's master list."

As a result of detailed reviews of each investment candidate by Wright's investment committee, some of the companies on the list were dropped for a variety of reasons. Before buying the remaining candidates, however, another decision hurdle had to be passed. According to Wright, "Quality is just one of the things we consider. The others are value and timing." The additional element of value was based on the extrapolation of probable future earnings on an absolute basis, as well as relative to other quality stocks. The timing issue took the action of the overall stock market into consideration.

Finally, Wright examined "the opinions of other investors toward a particular stock." He indicated that "people may be dead wrong, but their attitude is a fact. If it is negative or getting worse, it is wise to postpone buying."

The *Forbes* article sums up Wright's approach as "quality, value, timing. That's what he wants."

While an individual investor clearly could not duplicate the thoroughness inherent in Wright's quantitative and qualitative system, the basic tenets of his rating system provide a very relevant frame of reference for the investor. That frame of reference could no doubt have helped many an investor avoid huge losses in stocks that had been inflated by nothing more than hype in the 1990s, and that would never have had a chance of passing John Wright's rigorous screen. Neither the recommendations of the analysts nor the opinions of the investors that chased all of those fantasy stocks would have prevented these high fliers from flunking Wright's entrance exam.

Some further investment words of wisdom appeared in a January 1973 *Harvard Business Review* article by Peter L. Bernstein, chairman of Bernstein-Macauly, the investment management subsidiary of Hayden Stone Inc. (Hayden Stone, of course, was one of those venerable brokerage names that ultimately was absorbed in the rush of brokerage consolidations mentioned in Chapter 1.) That article was entitled "Advice to Managers: Watch earnings, not the ticker tape," and it noted that "management must not lose sight of what underlies a consistently high PE ratio: sustained high return on net worth."

Bernstein was quite correct in noting that "to most executives, a high price for the stock adds a meaningful sum to their personal wealth. To all companies, a high stock price makes external financing and acquisitions much easier and more profitable to consummate." Now, 30 years later, Bernstein would have been able to point to the incredible examples of executive bonuses and stock options that ranged into the hundreds of millions of dollars, and to the acquisition binges of companies like Cisco and Tyco, whose highly inflated stock prices served as wonderfully high currency that was eagerly accepted and prized by the acquired companies.

The article examines the performance of companies over a period of time and reaches the following conclusions:

1. A high P/E ratio is no guarantee of a good company or long-run stock performance.
2. Low P/Es don't protect against price declines.
3. For stock prices to go up, earnings must go up.
4. Return on book value is a good guide to both earnings and price performance.
5. Past corporate successes are only frail guides to future good fortune.
6. All stocks are "two-decision" stocks—no such thing as a "one-decision" stock exists.

That last reference to "two-decision" stocks refers, of course, to the fact that there is a time to buy and a time to sell. In his view, a "one-decision" buy-and-hold stock does not exist.

One has to wonder what Bernstein would have thought about those companies in the late 1990s that were selling at a multiple of loss, since he had questioned the reasonableness of "a perpetual 40 multiple." He resolved that latter issue in his own mind in the following way:

> If a company can double its earnings [over a 6 year period]—but needs 10 years before earnings double again—and perhaps 15 years the next time— then its PE ratio will fade with the passage of time. In other words, the price will rise more slowly than earnings. . . . Admittedly, pleasant surprises may come along . . . but 40 times earnings already anticipates [that].
>
> The issue becomes not whether its growth can be sustained, but whether its rate of growth can be sustained.

Investor enthusiasm during the stock market bubble apparently not only was based on the idea that companies could sustain their rate of growth, but in many cases depended on a continued expansion of that rate of growth—an expectation that proved to be very wrong.

Reviewing the Basics

There is no escaping the inevitable reality that earnings ultimately determine what an investor can reasonably be expected to pay for the purchase of either a business or its stock—as has been propounded by none other than Warren Buffett.

But leave it to Wall Street, Inc. to come up with a better idea—namely, buy stock in a company that is losing gobs of money in the hope that tomorrow's unlimited earnings potential will materialize. But tomorrow, in this way of thinking, is not meant to mean literally tomorrow—or even next year's tomorrow. In fact, these Delphi-like oracles are viewing really long-term prospects—by which time they will be pitching tomorrow's promise for another group of stocks.

During the bubble period, investors were constantly being reminded by analysts from big-name financial institutions that P/Es don't matter—that times had rendered that conventional thinking obsolete. That message was being repeated so often that investors began to believe it—much to their regret.

But the concept of a consistent record of real earnings, as contrasted to "pro forma non-earnings," does matter; income growth rates matter; balance sheets matter; profit margins and return on equity matters.

One fairly instructive way of thinking about PE levels involves the concept of "return on investment" (ROI), shown in Table 3.1.

Basically, ROI is the reciprocal of P/E. It means, for example, that if you purchased company XYZ at a P/E of 5, that company's earnings would provide you with a very attractive 20 percent annual return on your purchase price. But at a P/E of 20, the ROI is a modest 5 percent, and it drops to a minuscule 1 percent at a P/E multiple of 100.

Table 3.1   Return on Investment (ROI)

PE	ROI
5	20%
10	10%
20	5%
50	2%
100	1%

The business owner who borrowed money from a bank at 8 percent to finance the purchase of company XYZ at a P/E of 5 would clearly be enjoying profitability from the start—an ROI of 20 percent versus only 8 percent in interest cost. But the buyer of another company at a P/E of 100 would need to have deep pockets to subsidize the 7 percent difference between income and interest cost.

While a stockholder of a company is not confronted with concerns identical to those of an actual owner, investors would do well to heed Warren Buffett's advice to evaluate investment candidates just as if you were an owner. Therefore, the same investment criteria apply, whether one is considering the purchase of a company or just investing in its stock.

But beyond the fundamental measure of value as exemplified by P/E and ROI, it is the matter of compound income growth rate (CIGR) that, not surprisingly, attracts the attention of most investors. So while P/E by itself is often not highly regarded, a great deal of emphasis is placed on the concept of the P/E/CIGR ratio (commonly referred to as the PEG ratio), which indicates how much investors are willing to pay for income growth. The normal rule of thumb is that fair valuation is represented by a P/E level that is equal to the CIGR, providing a ratio of 1.

However, with the great emphasis on growth, analysts and money managers have promoted the suggestion that investors should be willing to value a stock at a PEG ratio of 2 or 3 and sometimes more. So, for example, investors are encouraged to believe that a company that is growing at a CIGR of 20 percent warrants a P/E of between 40 and 60. While for some that may not seem too high a price for a company with such good prospects, those high valuations could be vulnerable if the company's income growth rate were to falter.

During the aftermath of the bubble market, companies that had formerly posted 50 percent annual income gains saw earnings quickly transformed into losses—and in a declining market, investors became much less inclined to value stocks at unlimited multiples of losses.

The term *income growth rate* usually refers to a company's EPS growth rate. But first, the following shorthand way of viewing a company's EPS can help in analyzing a company's performance by focusing attention on two important EPS drivers.

$$\text{EPS} = \frac{\text{sales}}{\text{share}} \times \text{profit margin}$$

For example, a company with a sales/share ratio of 10 and a profit margin of 10 percent (or 0.1) would have an EPS of $1 per share—the same as that for another company with a sales/share ratio of 100 and a profit margin of 1 percent.

It is sales growth that tends to be the main long-term driver of EPS, primarily because profit margins are unlikely to consistently sustain meaningful gains. Over shorter intervals, however, profit margins can be pressured by adverse economic or business conditions, but then recover to more characteristic levels. In fact, if a company's valuation level has been marked down or adjusted to reflect a temporarily depressed profit margin, then the prospect for a significant snapback in earnings is a factor that should be examined and evaluated.

An analysis of the data for Coca-Cola (KO) in Table 3.2 and for Wal-Mart (WMT) in Table 3.3 provides an excellent insight into how helpful this concept can be in evaluating company performance.

The 5-year sales performance for KO shown in column 1 of Table 3.2 represents a very lackluster compound revenue growth rate of only 1.6 percent, which does little to support any impression that KO can be classified as a growth company. In contrast, however, Wal-Mart has been growing revenues at a brisk 16.6 percent clip.

The different nature of the two companies' business is indicated by the large discrepancy in both the sales/share and profit margin data shown in

Table 3.2 Performance Data for Coca-Cola (KO)

	(1) Sale ($ billions)	(2) Income ($ billions)	(3) Sales/Share	(4) Profit Margin (%)	(5) EPS
1997	18.9	4.13	7.60	21.9	1.64
1998	18.8	3.53	7.57	18.8	1.42
1999	19.8	2.43	7.97	12.3	0.98
2000	20.5	2.18	8.23	10.6	0.88
2001	20.1	3.97	8.09	19.8	1.60

Table 3.3 Performance Data for Wal-Mart (WMT)

	(1) Sale ($ billions)	(2) Income ($ billions)	(3) Sales/Share	(4) Profit Margin (%)	(5) EPS
1997	117	3.53	26.50	2.99	0.78
1998	138	4.43	3.92	3.22	0.99
1999	165	5.38	37.07	3.26	1.25
2000	191	6.30	42.98	3.29	1.40
2001	218	6.67	48.93	3.06	1.49

the two tables. KO's low sales/share numbers are accompanied by exceptionally high after-tax profit margins, whereas WMT is characterized by high sales/share and relatively low profit margins.

As can be observed, KO suffered sharply declining profit margins over the 1998–2000 3-year period, which dramatically affected its EPS. WMT's profit margins, on the other hand, have remained relatively stable, with EPS growth coming primarily from revenue growth. This view of both companies clearly helps in evaluating their prospects.

Given this, it is an amazing coincidence that both KO and WMT were at a price of $54 per share and at an exact P/E of 35.80 on May 30, 2002.

The data suggest that KO's profit margin is unlikely to advance much beyond the 20 percent range; as a result, future EPS gains will depend entirely on revenue growth, which will have to do much better than 1.6 percent to support the current P/E.

Wal-Mart's revenue growth rates of 15.9 percent and 13.9 percent in the past 2 years are below its 4-year compound average of 16.6 percent. In addition, a slight drop in profit margins in 2001 pressured its EPS gain. For the most part, however, WMT's EPS gain will be a function of revenue growth.

Based on this rather limited analysis, it would appear that both stocks can be considered to be fully valued on a PEG basis. In fact, if an analyst or investor were to examine KO's income record without knowing that it was for Coca-Cola, it is rather unlikely that she or he would value such a stock at a P/E of 35.80.

In Wal-Mart's case, the stock is valued at twice its 4-year EPS growth rate of 17.6 percent, but note should be taken of the fact that its 2-year growth rate has been a subpar 9.2 percent.

While the concept of calculating a company's PEG ratio is very valid, it is subject to significant practical problems in the real world. A calculation of KO's 4-year CIGR would be negative, while its 1-year growth rate would be 82 percent—neither of which is truly representative for KO.

In this regard, there is a case in which the EPS of a high-profile technology company was reported as being 252 percent above year-ago levels. The number was trumpeted over and over on CNBC, and was featured in the *Wall Street Journal* story covering the earnings release. But that amazing performance represented an EPS increase from $0.01 to $0.03 per share. The use of percentage changes in instances like that seem to be aimed at producing dramatic impact, and certainly have nothing to do with fundamentals—nor should they be used in calculating a company's CIGR.

The plain fact of the matter is that unless a company's growth rate is somewhat consistent, calculation of 3-year, 5-year, or even 10-year CIGRs can be extremely dependent on the starting and ending points of those calculations.

The difficulty in determining a truly representative CIGR is illustrated by Table 3.4, which gives an example for 3M that clearly indicates how significant the starting point of the CIGR calculation can be.

Column 2 lists the year-to-year simple percentage changes for the column 1 EPS data. Column 3 represents the CIGR for each indicated year, calculated by using 1997 as the base period (or starting point), while the column 4 CIGR values are calculated using 1998 as the base period. Column 5 lists the midpoint values of 3M's annual P/E range.

For 3M, a huge inconsistency in CIGR values, as indicated by columns 3 and 4, resulted from the 1-year shift in the base period from 1997 to 1998. Selecting or arbitrarily using any of the numbers in columns 3 or 4 without clearly putting them in perspective would obviously be quite misleading.

From an investing vantage point, the 1997–2002 average P/E for 3M of approximately 25 could be interpreted as having been fairly generous when contrasted to the company's rather lackluster CIGR record.

The results of computer screening programs that rely on compound income growth rates should be carefully checked, since company growth rate comparisons may not be truly representative—as the 3M example illustrates. A similar problem exists in reports published in business and financial magazines that rank companies by income growth rates, or that simply list the growth rate along with other company data.

The format of Table 3.4 is recommended as part of any review of companies of interest.

One very straightforward and convenient way in which to correlate P/E levels and income growth rates on a quarterly basis is illustrated in

Table 3.4 Compound Income Growth Rate (CIGR) Calculation for 3M

	(1) EPS	(2) % Change	(3) CIGR (%), 1997 Base	(4) CIGR (%), 1998 Base	(5) P/E (Midpoint of Annual Range)
1997	5.06				18
1998	2.97	(41)	(41)		27
1999	4.34	46	(8)	46	20
2000	4.64	7	(3)	25	22
2001	3.58	(23)	(9)	6	30
August 2002	3.95	10	(5)	7	32

Table 3.5   Quarterly EPS, Growth, and P/E Data for Hadco Corp.

(1) Calendar Quarterly	(2) Quarterly EPS	(3) % Change from Year-ago Quarter	(4) Trailing Year EPS	(5) Quarterly-End Price	(6) Trailing Year P/E	(7) PEG Ratio
Sept. 1993	0.14	−22%		8.00		
Dec.	0.22	−4%	0.76	8.50	11.2	
Mar. 1994	0.10	−33%	0.73	7.50	10.3	
June	0.22	−12%	0.68	6.50	9.5	
Sep.	0.27	+93%	0.81	7.75	9.5	
Dec.	0.34	+55%	0.93	9.00	9.7	0.44
Mar. 1995	0.29	+190%	1.12	12.00	10.7	
June	0.49	+123%	1.39	25.00	18.0	
Sep.	0.56	+107%	1.68	28.00	16.7	
Dec.	0.63	+85%	1.97	28.00	14.2	0.33
Mar. 1996	0.65	+124%	2.33	30.00	12.9	
June	0.71	+45%	2.55	22.00	8.6	
Sep.	0.72	+29%	2.71	32.00	11.8	
Dec.	0.81	+29%	2.89	46.00	15.9	0.34
Mar. 1997	0.81	+25%	3.05	40.00	13.1	
June	0.91	+28%	3.25	65.00	20.0	

Table 3.5. The table was constructed using only quarterly EPS data and end-of-quarter stock prices for Hadco Corp.

Although Hadco was acquired several years ago, it provides an instructive example of how an investor can approach and utilize fundamental analysis. The following narrative describes my personal participation and involvement with Hadco from an investment perspective.

The first inklings of the impending pickup in the technology sector began to surface in the spring of 1994. I had made a practice of requesting investor relations packages for companies that might be of interest. In addition, I asked to be placed on the mailing list for quarterly and annual company reports. This was intended to provide me with a convenient and disciplined approach to monitoring business conditions for a number of companies in various industries.

As I was reviewing a batch of new quarterly reports, the Hadco Corp. April 30, 1994, report to stockholders struck a responsive cord, prompting a more thorough review of the company's latest annual report. The corporate profile description stated:

> Hadco Corporation is a leading supplier of electronic inter-connect products and services. Markets served include original equipment manufac-

turers and contract assemblers in the computer, telecommunications, automotive, medical instruments and industrial automation sector of the electronics industry.

Hadco basically produced printed circuit multilayer boards upon which electronic components are mounted. What is significant about the board business is that these completed board assemblies are an indispensable part of all electronic products. In effect, the prospect for printed circuit board makers like Hadco would closely track the growth of the entire electronics industry.

In its second-quarter interim report for the period ending April 30, 1994, Hadco reported a slight EPS decline to $0.22 versus the previous year's $0.25. However, one attention-getting item in the report indicated that

> Bookings for the quarter were a record $70.1 million, up 44% from the same period a year ago.

The company had a very strong balance sheet, with $24 million in cash equivalents and a low debt-to-equity ratio of 15.6 percent. Full-year 1993 EPS had been $0.76, the book value approximated $7 per share, and the stock was selling at $6.50 per share. After I purchased a token amount of stock, it drifted to the $6 level (Figure 3.1), and I bought more stock. At that point I contacted the CFO, and he referred me to an analyst's April 13, 1994, report from a Boston-based brokerage firm, which concluded that

> We continue to believe that Hadco must articulate a long-term strategy for increasing sales and profits in ways that do not depend on uncontrollable variables, such as short-term swings in demand.

What an astounding revelation! The report summarized as follows:

> Until investors gain confidence that management can formulate and execute such a strategy, the stock will struggle.

The analyst's hold rating was somewhat discouraging, but the company's report of substantially higher bookings tended to offset the analyst's misgivings.

In an attempt to gain some firsthand perspective, I again called the CFO and arranged a brief meeting that would include a tour of the company's Salem, New Hampshire, facilities. Its facilities were impressive, as was the range of products being produced for a customer base that had grown from 180 in 1991 to about 300. And, indeed, the plant and its production lines seemed to be buzzing with activity.

FIGURE 3.1   Hadco Price Chart

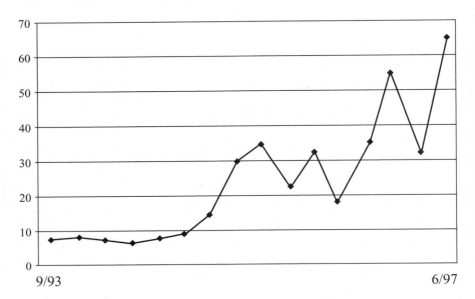

Based on that visit, I made my final purchases of stock, restrained to some extent by the analyst's reservations. The analyst had projected an EPS of $0.70 for 1994 and $0.85 for 1995. The actual results were $0.93 and $1.98, respectively. Earnings peaked at $2.89 in 1996 before declining in 1997 and 1998.

By January 1995, as analysts began to recognize the positive trends that were emerging in the electronics industry, Hadco stock had risen to $9.50. In April, a number of brokerage firms issued "strong buy" recommendations for a group of electronic companies, including Hadco. As this flurry of interest in the sector increased, the Boston analyst issued a new report that now contained a strong buy rating for Hadco at a price of $12 per share.

In June the stock reached $17, and by September it had reached $30. It had been a great run, but I decided to take the long-term gain. The company continued to do well, and I bought it again in March 1996, when the stock dropped to $22, and again sold it at about $30. I bought the stock again in July when it dropped to $19, and sold it in December at $54.

While those last two trades represented short-term gains, I made the decision not to hold for the long-term capital gains prospects because of Hadco's high price volatility, which was obviously being generated by institutions that traded almost exclusively on the basis of price momentum.

Apparently the professional money managers were warming up for the really big momentum game that was to come.

While Hadco had had a strong balance sheet and above-average profit margins over the years and was selling at a reasonable valuation, in 1994 it was the potential for significantly higher prospective sales that made the difference in my decision to buy the stock at that time.

The most instructive starting point in reviewing Table 3.5 is the column 3 calculation, which represents the percentage change in quarterly EPS versus year-ago levels. The first four comparisons in column 3 for Hadco are negative, and those results are reflected in the price decline, as indicated in column 5. But as noted, Hadco had reported a substantial increase in order bookings, which, indeed, were reflected in a positive 93 percent EPS comparison in the subsequent quarter.

In general, when the column 3 values switch from a negative pattern to a positive one, or from positive to negative, the price of the stock can usually be expected to respond accordingly.

Hadco's quarterly earnings comparisons remained extremely positive for the last 12 quarters shown—and its stock price responded quite nicely to that trend.

Hadco achieved consecutive annual earnings gains of 22 percent, 112 percent, and 47 percent for 1994 to 1996, well above its trailing year (TRYR) P/Es (column 6), which resulted in a column 7 PEG ratio of well under 1 for those years.

The information summarized by this table format is extremely helpful in assessing a company's performance, and its use is strongly recommended in analyzing or monitoring all stocks of interest.

Whether one is considering purchasing a company or just investing in its stock, other financial items that should be examined in addition to earnings include (1) debt-equity ratio, (2) cash flow, and (3) capital spending requirements.

Attention must also be directed to issues such as

1. Management depth and experience
2. Product growth potential
3. Competitive environment
4. General industry prospects

It may seem that investing need not get this complicated, but the objective of going through these evaluation checklists is to uncover any potentially negative factors that could change your opinion of the company.

One difficulty confronting the individual, in contrast to the professional money manager, is the different frame of reference that each applies to investment decision making.

One would normally assume that actual earnings results were to be taken to mean what they said—losses would not really be good news and would not be expected to augur well for a stock's price performance.

However, the new age mentality has revised that thinking to an approach that compares reported results to Wall Street's expectations. So if a company beats the financial community's projections of that loss by a single penny, that is great news that is trumpeted over and over again in a frenzy of celebration, hype, and higher prices for the stock.

The examples abound, but Teradyne (TER) will serve to illustrate the point. Teradyne's first quarter 2002 sales declined by 59 percent from the previous year's levels; the actual EPS loss was $0.42 per share, but it was $0.40 when certain costs were excluded. First Call estimates had been for a loss of $0.41, so TER beat Wall Street estimates by that much-revered penny, and the stock jumped by as much as $2.41 to $40.20 on trading of approximately 5 million shares.

Much to Wall Street's joy, the company reported an improving order trend and a decline in the number of cancellations, which would combine to reduce the second-quarter loss to only $0.31 per share.

Since the stock was well below its 2000 peak price of $115 per share, it must have appeared to be a bargain—current losses notwithstanding. But, then again, one has to be reminded that fund managers are investing other people's money. That celebratory rise in TER's stock price unfortunately proved to be short-lived, as the stock declined to $14 by the end of July 2002.

Motorola (MOT) is another case in point. In April 2002, MOT announced that it expected to record its sixth consecutive quarterly loss in its second quarter, as many of its business units were experiencing declining revenues.

The company had reported a first-quarter loss of $449 million, or $0.20 per share. However, MOT was projecting better "operating" earnings, excluding charges, as a result of cost-cutting measures, and the company hoped that it would reach "break-even" levels for the year as a whole. That "good news" was enough to result in a 9 percent jump in the price of MOT, as analysts expressed hope that Motorola's business appeared to be bouncing off the bottom. Not surprisingly, MOT subsequently gave back that 9 percent gain—and much more.

Both Teradyne and Motorola are strong competitors in their fields and may recover from the depressed business conditions that have been cited.

However, the question is not whether they will, at some point, once again achieve their previous income levels, but rather whether there are other investment candidates that are more attractive on a comparative basis.

The culture of Wall Street, Inc. is deeply ingrained, however, and mutual fund managers depend on the cover and support of analysts' upgrades, no matter how specious the reason. That's just the way the system works—fund managers are conditioned to respond to multiple ratings upgrades because they can all be winners—at least for a day or two.

For the individual investor, however, there does not seem to be any better alternative than following a disciplined approach that is based on thorough fundamental and technical analysis.

Using Technical Analysis Tools

Technical analysis is not nearly as complicated or forbidding as it may sound. It essentially consists of various methods of presenting and interpreting the meaning and implication of a stock's price action.

While many technical analysts make investment decisions based entirely upon their methods, the more conventional use of technical analysis is in attempting to confirm the conclusions arrived at on the basis of fundamental considerations. The idea is best reflected by John Wright's concern about "the opinion of others toward a particular stock." He worried that while "people may be dead wrong, their attitude is a fact." And that opinion is captured in the price action of a stock—which is why technical analysis is so very insightful and important.

There can be situations in which the fundamental considerations for a particular stock may seem compelling, but an element of caution is introduced by technical analysis. In such cases, it is important to satisfactorily resolve that discrepancy.

Among the various charting approaches to technical analysis, the use of moving averages represents an excellent starting point. Moving averages tend to work well primarily because of the tendency of price trends that are in motion to stay in motion, meaning that a downtrend or uptrend is very likely to sustain itself until the telltale signs of a reversal begin to form.

And moving-average lines help in identifying those extremely important turning points. Most technical analysts suggest the use of three moving averages of 50-, 100-, and 200-day durations, but any reasonable set of time periods can be utilized.

For long-term upward or downward trends, the 100-day and 200-day moving-average lines serve as critical support or resistance levels. The shorter 50-day average becomes more important at major turning points. The example in Figure 3.2 illustrates how the interaction of the three lines helps in the investment decision-making process.

What generally happens at important bottoms, for example, is that the stock price begins to fluctuate around the 50-day line, but remains well below the 100- and 200-day lines. As that process continues, the 50-day line will flatten out and even begin to increase. That positive sign, however, does not completely confirm the existence of a bottom. But when the 50-day line crosses the 100-day line, it is usually a very positive signal that an important uptrend is being established.

That fact is more convincingly confirmed when the 100-day line crosses the 200-day line. For investors who are favorably inclined toward a stock based on fundamentals, the first crossing of the 100-day line by the 50-day line is often sufficient to initiate purchases.

During the upward trend, it is vitally important that the price of the stock remain above the 100- and 200-day lines, since the price levels of the lines are considered to represent important "support." As long as the stock price does not break below those support levels, the upward trend remains intact. The first sign of a top reversal, however, is noted by a rolling over by the 50-day line, presaging the beginning of a downward trend in which the moving-average lines will represent price resistance instead of support.

Figure 3.3, a price chart for Solectron (SLR), provides an excellent representation of the value of moving averages in evaluating underlying stock price trends.

Solectron's price stayed well above both the 100- and 200-day moving averages throughout 1999, but as the stock began an obvious sideways trad-

FIGURE 3.2   Interaction of 50-, 100-, and 200-Day Moving Averages at Turning Points

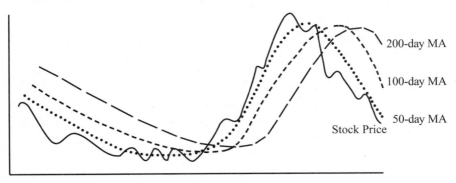

FIGURE 3.3 **Solectron Price Chart with Moving-Average Lines**

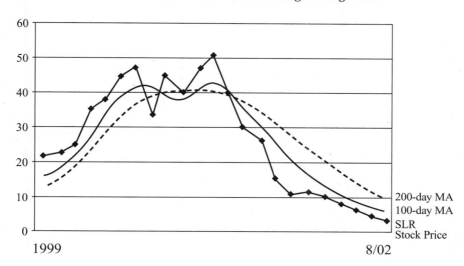

ing pattern, both moving-average lines also flattened out. The 100-day moving-average line, which crossed the 200-day line in the spring of 2000, gave the first indication of a potential downside move, which was convincingly confirmed by another crossing at the beginning of 2001 with the stock at $40 per share. That very clear "sell" signal remained intact as the stock declined to the $4 level—during which time it consistently remained below its 100-day and 200-day moving average lines.

Point-and-figure (P&F) charting represents another interesting approach that can be used to validate conclusions based on moving-average analysis. The example shown in Figure 3.4 helps to explain the P&F methodology.

The O and X symbols represent down and up moves in a stock's price. Each price "box" generally represents $1/2$ point for stocks below $20 per share and a full point for higher-priced stocks.

In effect, then, it is price movement alone that establishes this chart—there is no timeline as in a conventional price chart. Any recorded move in price, however, has to amount to a three-box price change. For example, the price of XYZ's stock must drop to $28 before the first three O's are recorded in the chart. Another O is recorded for every additional single-box drop in price, until there is a subsequent three-box upward move, as depicted in the third column of Figure 3.4.

The interpretation of P&F charts is as follows:

FIGURE 3.4   Point-and-Figure Chart for Stock XYZ

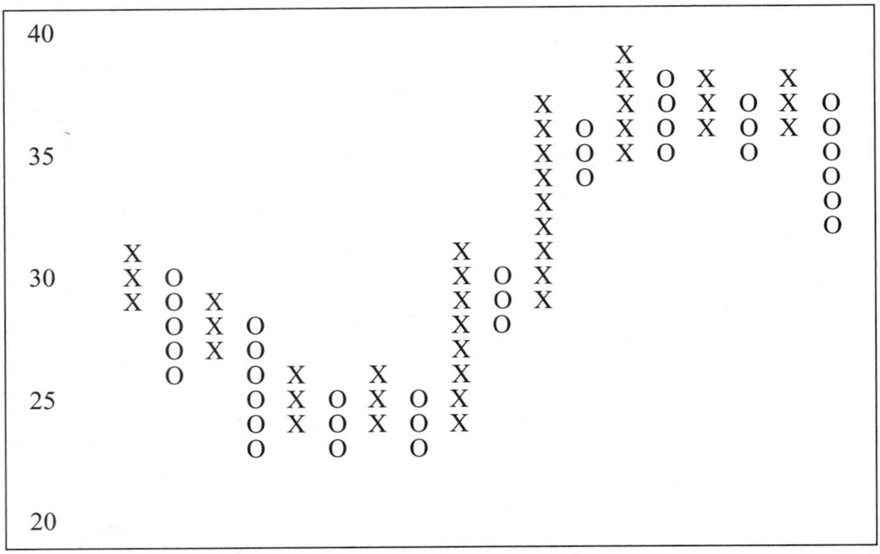

1. Bottoms are usually signaled by what is called a successful test of a "triple bottom" formation that consists of three O's, such as registered for XYZ at a price of $23.

2. An important upside breakout is indicated when the "triple top" formation as represented by the three X's at $26 is exceeded.

3. Tops are identified when the rally mode consisting of a pattern of higher X's and higher O's falters, finally resulting in the breaching of the $35 triple bottom.

It should be noted that there are a number of other chart pattern variations that analysts look for. An interesting feature of the point-and-figure charts provided by StockCharts.com is that they identify significant positive or negative patterns as they develop.

Another popular measure that serves as a useful indicator of a stock's overall performance is referred to as a relative strength index (RSI). This seeks to measure how much better or worse a particular stock is doing as compared to other stocks or indices. There are services that provide numerical measures of RSI, but one very practical and convenient approach to checking relative strength is to use online charting capabilities such as those that are available at NASDAQ.com and Bloomberg.com.

FIGURE 3.5   Indexed Chart Comparing Solectron and M/I Schottenstein Price Performance

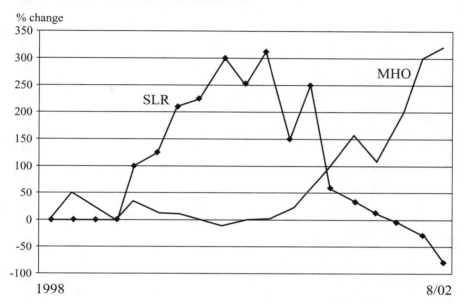

A relative strength measure that compares the performance of two stocks is illustrated by the 5-year comparative performance of Solectron (SLR) versus M/I Schottenstein Homes (MHO), as shown in Figure 3.5. It clearly depicts the preference for the new economy over the old economy during the bubble phase, and the subsequent complete reversal of that trend when the bubble began to burst.

Charting techniques should be considered as tools of the trade, and investors should consider the advantages of utilizing the most appropriate tools available.

The Importance of Sector Analysis

Most investors are familiar with reports of stock market action characterized by "sector rotation"—namely, the movement of institutional money from one industry sector to another. If cyclical stocks are reported to likely benefit from an improving economy, cyclicals are bought en masse and some other industry is sold. If a potential cancer cure is intimated, drugs would be bought—possibly at the expense of cyclicals.

Much of that action tends to be tactical in nature as fund managers seek to capitalize on one development or another, and those short-term reactions can generally be ignored by the average investor. But industry sectors do, in fact, periodically experience significant fundamental changes in their outlook, and it is this type of development with longer-term implications that the investor must recognize. If any indications of industry sector weakness emerge, all stocks in that sector can generally be expected to react as a group.

In many respects, selecting the right industry sector to invest in can be more important than deciding which of the companies within the sector are better situated. That is not to diminish the importance of company selection, but companies are obviously more likely to prosper under favorable than under unfavorable industry conditions.

Selecting the best-situated industries, however, is more easily said than done. Developing an overview and a basic understanding of all the industry sectors that constitute the economy is a fairly daunting task, but it also is a critically important one.

The nine major industry sector groupings and the 47 broadly defined industry sectors listed in Table 3.6 each represent a significant slice of the nation's economic pie—and as such, they provide a useful point of departure for conducting a comparative analysis of industry sectors. The significance of Table 3.6 is that it essentially defines the industry sector universe available to the investor.

In the process of assimilating business and financial news and developments that affect companies and industries, the investor should periodically refer back to Table 3.6. In addition, the investor should consider establishing an industry priority list that can become the basis for initiating a comparative analysis of selected industries. That practice is likely to help the investor focus more sharply on particular industry sectors, which in turn will serve to stimulate further research efforts. Ultimately, over a period of time, this fund of accumulated industry sector knowledge will help the investor develop an added degree of confidence—and, more important, the ability to make more informed investment decisions.

Essentially, the Hadco example previously discussed earlier in this chapter under "Reviewing the Basics" was both a company and an industry story. Initially it was the company news release that provided the early signal of a developing industry upturn. Within 6 months, it was becoming apparent that a sustainable improvement in business conditions for the electronics industry was materializing, and investor interest in the industry increased rather dramatically. Based on what was going on in the industry, I bought two other board makers—both later acquired by Hadco.

TABLE 3.6 Industry Sector Groupings

1. *Consumer-Related*	Office Equipment
Apparel	Semiconductors
Cosmetics	Telecom Equipment
Drugs	
Food & Beverages	6. *Energy & Natural Resources*
Footware	Oil
Household Supplies	Metals
2. *Manufacturing*	7. *Construction-Related*
Autos & Parts	Building Materials and Lumber
Chemicals	Homebuilding
Machinery	Home Furnishings
Paper	
Steel	8. *Services*
Textiles	Advertising
	Broadcasting
3. *Retail Stores*	Computer Software & Services
Department	Entertainment
Drug	Financial Services
Grocery	Food Services
Specialty	Healthcare
	Lodging
4. *Finance*	Oil Industry Services
Banks	Publishing
Brokerage & Investment Banking	Restaurants
Insurance	
	9. *Transportation and Utilities*
5. *Technology*	Airlines
Aerospace & Defense	Gas & Electric Utilities
Computers	Railroads
Electronic Components & Equipment	Trucking
Medical & Scientific Equipment	Water Utilities

This was a strategy of concentrating in an industry and diversifying to some extent within that industry sector, much like the example of investing in the homebuilders in 1999–2000. At one point the top 15 homebuilders had a combined market capitalization of only $6 to $7 billion and were valued at average P/Es in the 4 to 5 range at a time when individual high-flying stocks with huge losses were being valued at many tens of billion of dollars.

Another example of an industry sector play involved the savings bank industry in the early 1990s.

By 1992, the S&L crisis had essentially run its course, and there were hopeful indications that the economy was going in the right direction. However, banks badly needed the opportunity to improve the quality of their balance sheets, and the Federal Reserve's low interest-rate policy was just what the banking industry needed. The resulting lower cost of money served to widen margin spreads and increase earnings. In addition, the low rates helped the real estate market begin its recovery, thus enabling the banks to work down their problem loans.

While it is true that low interest rates tend to favor borrowers over savers, the larger Federal Reserve imperative was based on the fact that economic prosperity could not materialize without a financially sound banking system.

It was after recognizing the clear signal that savings institutions would soon be on a path to recovery that I invested in a number of thrifts, including names such as Home Federal of Missouri, West Mass Bankshares, Maryland Federal, and Grove Bank—all institutions that were subsequently acquired.

The decision to concentrate investments in that particular sector is an example of a situation in which such an approach may be appropriate. Again, it should be emphasized that this was a case of industry concentration and company diversification within that industry. Fortunately, there were hundreds of small publicly traded savings institutions to choose from at the time, and diversification increased the probability that one or more of them might be acquired, as proved to be the case.

From a broader perspective, specific opportunities like that involving the savings bank sector often develop as a result of a particular and sometimes unique set of circumstances that may not be replicated in the same way in the future. In order to be in a position to take advantage of such opportunities when they arise, the investor must stay informed and remain particularly alert to shifting economic, industry sector, and company developments.

The Influence of Economic Factors

At the outset, let it be acknowledged that it is much easier to analyze what the economy has done than what it is going to do. Not even the Federal Reserve's legions of analysts and researchers—who have all the data that one could ever want at their disposal—are very good at economic forecasting. That often leaves the Fed's illustrious chairman, Alan Greenspan, in the awkward position of having to discuss the state of the economy in terms of "on the one hand—but on the other hand." When Greenspan boasts that the Federal Reserve's economic models are the best in the world, he conveniently avoids making any reference to their forecasting accuracy.

Basically, economic models are constructed by back-testing historical data to determine what particular variables are "highly correlated" with actual results. For example, it would not be surprising to find that housing starts are highly dependent on both interest rates and the unemployment rate. In essence, then, all that has to be done is to forecast interest rates and the unemployment rate, and there you have it: a housing-starts forecast. That, however, simply transfers the burden to the forecasting of two other economic variables that are equally as hard to pin down. No wonder, then, that economic forecasting is often considered more of an art than a science.

One of the most erroneous theoretical relationships, which was at the heart of Federal Reserve policy for many years, stemmed from the fact that the Fed's models had consistently indicated that inflationary pressures would inevitably build in the economy if the unemployment rate were to drop below 6 percent. Any Federal Reserve action based on that assumption would obviously have had a serious impact on the economy. But, as it turned out, as the unemployment rate dropped below 5 percent and then below 4 percent, the much-feared prospect of escalating inflation rates did not materialize. Fortunately, in this instance, the Fed took its cue from the benign inflation data instead of from its models.

Those models most likely did not fully capture the impact of the developing global economy. Manufacturing jobs have continued to decline as the trend to offshore outsourcing continues at a steady and unrelenting pace. In the past, labor constraints would have tended to create inflationary pressures, but the new reality was that the United States began to benefit from an almost unlimited—and cheaper—global workforce.

For the most part, the state of the economy can be summarized in just one word: jobs. In 1982, the unemployment rate reached 11 percent—the economy was very bad. In early 2000, the unemployment rate was under 4 percent—the economy was very good.

In the early 1980s, in an attempt to get people back to work, the Reagan administration utilized the deficit-spending powers of government to engineer an economic recovery. One may choose to call it "the $5 trillion solution," but a protracted period of economic stagnation did not seem like much of an alternative. The economics of the situation was very simple—increase demand by getting spending money into the hands of consumers, and job creation will follow.

That $5 trillion shot in the arm worked wonders, but even the world's largest economy would probably have trouble borrowing that much money if it needed to do so in the future. At some point, lenders get more con-

cerned about the eventual return of their capital than about their current
return on capital.

A much different scenario developed in the mid-1990s. Not much was
happening in the economy until technology-related spending got a big boost
from Internet and telecom start-ups and corporate information systems
upgrades. This new-economy spending easily added an incremental $2 tril-
lion to the economy over a very short period of time—funded not by the
government, but by willing and anxious investors and investment banks.

Again, all of that extra spending did wonders for the economy—and
companies were expanding so rapidly that they could not find enough
workers to handle their projected needs.

In evaluating the implications that flow from these defining episodes,
two conclusions stand out:

1. Had it not been for heavy deficit spending in the 1980s, economic
    recovery from the 1982 recession would have been far more tenuous.
2. The 1990s boom would also not have developed as it did without
    the huge incremental spending that occurred.

In looking ahead, one has to wonder who will provide the next multi-
trillion-dollar influx of money to support economic growth beyond typical
"real" GDP levels in the 2.5 to 3.5 percent range.

In general, investors can follow the major forces at play in the economy
without getting deeply mired in economic statistics. But, that being said, a
basic understanding of how the economy works is necessary for recognizing developing trends—and their implications for the stock market.

Investors can derive most of what they need in order to stay informed
by monitoring the government economic releases in the *Wall Street Journal*
and in *BusinessWeek*. Over time, familiarity with the data will grow and
will take on more meaning.

But where economic statistics are concerned, less is sometimes better.
It is in that vein that the following limited list of government releases that
deserve to be monitored is presented. Eventually, certain statistics will take
on added meaning, as discussed here.

1. *Unemployment rate and job creation numbers.* The monthly
    unemployment number (released on the first Friday of each
    month) is accompanied by a job creation number. It usually takes
    the creation of about 200,000 jobs each month just to maintain a
    given unemployment rate, because of new entrants to the labor
    force.

Detail within the job creation number indicates how many jobs were gained or lost in several sectors including manufacturing, services, construction, government, and so on. This breakdown can be helpful in properly interpreting the data when, for example, strength in certain sectors is offset by weakness in others.

The Labor Department employment report that is printed in the *Wall Street Journal* is useful in that it provides actual labor force and unemployment levels in addition to the usual unemployment rate in percent.

2. *Weekly unemployment claims.* This number (released each Thursday) represents the number of new claims filed for the most recent week. It should be pointed out that only some 40 percent of the workforce is covered by unemployment insurance, with the others being ineligible to file. A companion statistic provides "continuing claims" statistics, which in mid-2002 was at a 19-year high of 3.9 million.

Weekly "new claims" numbers of about 350,000 generally would indicate a stable unemployment rate; numbers in the 400,000 and above range imply an increasing unemployment rate; and numbers in the 300,000 range would generally result in a declining unemployment rate.

3. *Gross domestic product (GDP).* The GDP number is intended to represent the sum of all economic activity in "real" or constant dollar terms—namely, excluding the inflation component. GDP data are released quarterly and given on a seasonally adjusted annual rate basis. The quarterly numbers are often subject to significant revisions, but on an annual basis the economy generally conforms to a long-term sustainable GDP growth rate that is in the 2.5 to 3.5 percent range.

4. *Consumer price index (CPI) and producer price index (PPI).* The lower these figures are, the better—hopefully, they are below 2.5 percent on an annual year-over-year basis. However, these numbers are reported on a monthly basis, so that an average monthly number of 0.2 percent would be required to meet the 2.5 percent limit. Both the CPI and the PPI include the volatile food and energy components. A separately reported "core" rate for each excludes the food and energy sectors.

The PPI concentrates on prices for raw goods and the cost of "intermediate" goods. It is intended to provide indications of incipient inflation in the goods-producing sector of the economy. The same limits as for the CPI would be considered acceptable.

5. *Personal income and spending.* These are significant numbers in that personal consumption basically drives the economy. They are generally quoted as month-to-month changes. A 6 percent annual average increase for both in nominal terms is a reasonable expectation.

6. *Durable goods orders.* Monthly durable goods orders represent a very volatile series that is subject to dramatic revisions as a result of end-of-month orders for large items such as aircraft. In spite of that deficiency, the longer-term trend of durable goods orders serves as a proxy for the strength of business investment trends.

7. *Industrial production and capacity utilization.* The recent weakness that has characterized the manufacturing sector since mid-2000 has resulted in a capacity utilization rate of only 75 percent versus a more normal level that approximates 82 percent.

The remaining group of suggested economic statistics to monitor provide additional information that can be helpful in analyzing economic trends.

8. *Housing starts.*

9. *Auto sales.*

10. *Capital spending projections.*

11. *Interest rates.*

12. *Federal budget—deficit versus surplus.*

When the economy is in an expansion mode, everything seems to go right. However, it is in less certain times that the forces on the economy tend to take on greater significance.

In those instances, the use of Figure 3.6 might be helpful. It depicts the economy as a closed circle that iterates upon itself as follows:

Weekly unemployment claims (1) foreshadow the month's unemployment and job creation data (2), which influence consumer income and spending (3), which affect GDP (4), possibly putting pressure on the CPI (5), which then would influence Federal Reserve interest-rate policy (6), which in turn influences the weekly unemployment claims, thereby initiating a new iteration.

In the past, the major jolts to the economy developed either as a result of the inflationary impact of rising oil prices or because of higher interest rates that were part of a Federal Reserve–induced slowdown.

One additional factor shown in Figure 3.6 is indicated as an "exogenous wild card"—namely, any unanticipated major development like an oil embargo or a September 11–type of incident.

FIGURE 3.6   The Economic Closed Circle

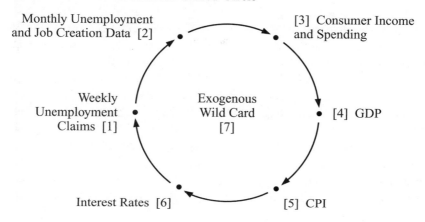

Monthly Unemployment and Job Creation Data [2]

[3] Consumer Income and Spending

Weekly Unemployment Claims [1]

Exogenous Wild Card [7]

[4] GDP

Interest Rates [6]

[5] CPI

One final significant and worrisome statistic that bears careful attention is the performance of the U.S. trade deficit, which now approximates 4 percent of GDP and has been projected to rise to 6.5 percent in the next 4 to 5 years.

While economic statistics tend to fall below some investors' radar screen, it may be well to consider the fact that it is the condition of the economy that ultimately influences the stock market—not the other way around, as some would suggest.

Stocks versus Market Averages

Divining company and industry fundamentals is one thing, but trying to figure out the level at which the market averages should trade is quite a different matter. That is not to say that some don't try—highly paid strategists at investment firms, for example. But their prognostications often tend to lack the level of justification that would inspire confidence.

When the market was soaring in the late 1990s, it was fashionable for these strategists to make headlines with their bold predictions. The market accommodated those who were playing that game for a while—until it decided not to.

The boldest and also the most outlandish of these market views was captured by James K. Glassman's book *Dow 36,000*. In this book, Glassman argued that P/E levels of 100 made eminently good sense. His views, though far beyond the mainstream, succeeded in attracting attention, and he has often shared his insights as a guest on the business news shows.

But *Dow 36,000* begs an important question: Is that the projection for the "good Dow," the "average Dow," or the "not-so-good Dow"?

In fact, the disparity in the 5-year stock price performances of the 30 DJIA stocks (as of August 8, 2002) as indicated by Table 3.7 clearly supports the notion that the DJIA is far from a solid monolith.

The compilation in Table 3.7 divides the listing into groups of 10 Dow stocks, ranked by descending order of 5-year percentage gains.

As indicated, the top 10 "good Dow" stocks appreciated by an average of 55.2 percent over 5 years, or at a 9.2 percent annual compound growth rate. The next 10 "average Dow" stocks had a modest average loss (−4.4 percent) and a negative compound growth rate (−0.9 percent). But a full third of the Dow components, the "not-so-good Dow" group of stocks, performed rather badly, with a dismal average loss (−40.4 percent) and a significant average compound decline (−9.8 percent).

That huge level of discrepancy in performance is further exacerbated by the generally inconsistent patterns shown by both (1) the company stock charts themselves and (2) the comparison of each company's graph to that of the DJIA over the 5-year period.

A 5-year summary of the three major indices, shown in Table 3.8, reveals how unrewarding the stock market has been for an extended period of time. While the fact that NASDAQ's performance was significantly worse than that of its counterparts comes as no surprise, the relatively better showing by the DJIA as compared to the S&P 500 may have more to do with the way the DJIA is calculated. In making comparisons between the three major indices, it is important to note the following differences that exist in their structure:

1. The DJIA is a price-weighted index that is obtained by summing the prices of the 30 stocks and dividing that total by a divisor (currently about 6.918), which is modified to adjust for stock splits and other changes, including company substitutions.

    One obvious drawback of the DJIA is the fact that its 30 stocks provide what might be considered to be a limited statistical sample. Another issue is that price weighting effectively places greater weight on higher-priced stocks.

2. The S&P 500 is a market-capitalization-weighted index obtained by summing the market values of the 500 stocks; the total is then modified by its own adjustment factor.

    Having 500 companies in the index allows for broad industry representation. However, the index is subject to being unduly affected by a small number of high-valuation stocks.

Table 3.7   Ranked 5-Year Price Performance of the 30 DJIA Stocks (August 8, 2002)

	5-Year Price Gain (%)	5-Year CIGR (%)
The "Good Dow" Index (Top 10 Dow Stocks)		
1. Wal-Mart	163.7	21.4
2. Home Depot	72.4	11.5
3. Johnson & Johnson	72.0	11.4
4. United Technologies	60.0	9.9
5. Microsoft	33.9	6.0
6. General Electric	33.5	6.0
7. Citigroup	33.3	5.9
8. IBM	32.1	5.7
9. 3M	31.4	5.6
10. American Express	19.4	3.6
Average	55.2	9.2
The "Average Dow" Index (Middle 10 Dow Stocks)		
11. Procter & Gamble	18.4	3.4
12. Alcoa	15.3	2.9
13. ExxonMobil	7.8	1.5
14. Philip Morris	6.3	1.2
15. Merck	−4.5	−0.9
16. McDonald's	−11.1	−2.3
17. SBC	−11.9	−2.5
18. General Motors	−12.9	−2.7
19. Intel	−24.3	−5.4
20. Caterpillar	−27.3	−6.2
Average	−4.4	−0.9
The "Not-So-Good Dow" Index (Bottom 10 Dow Stocks)		
21. Coca-Cola	−28.6	−6.5
22. Boeing	−29.7	−6.8
23. Honeywell	−30.9	−7.1
24. International Paper	−33.3	−7.8
25. J. P. Morgan	−35.8	−8.5
26. DuPont	−38.5	−9.3
27. Disney	−48.2	−12.3
28. AT&T	−50.1	−13.0
29. Hewlett-Packard	−52.0	−13.7
30. Eastman Kodak	−56.7	−15.4
Average	−40.4	−9.8

**Table 3.8   5-Year Summary of the Major Market Average
(August 8, 2002, Close)**

	5-Year Gain (%)	5-Year CIGR (%)
DJIA	+3.2%	+0.6%
S&P 500	−7.4%	−1.5%
NASDAQ	−19.7%	−4.3%

3.   The NASDAQ also is a market-capitalization-weighted index, with
      its universe containing all listed NASDAQ stocks. While the NAS-
      DAQ index consists of several thousand companies, it also suffers
      from an inordinate influence of high-capitalization companies.

Since the DJIA consists of only 30 stocks, the task of contrasting the
performance of the DJIA using the conventional price-weighted structure
against a market-capitalization version of the DJIA is not very difficult.
Calculations have indicated a generally close approximation for most periods, except when unusual strength or weakness develops in the high-cap
companies in the DJIA.

Since the 10 DJIA stocks with the highest market cap would dominate
a market-capitalization version of the DJIA, the significant weakness in a
number of these stocks during the year ending in August 2, 2002, would
probably have resulted in a market-capitalization-weighted version of the
DJIA that more closely approximated the performance of the S&P 500.

While the level at which the major averages trade is important primarily
for those who invest in index funds, or funds that mimic the averages, there
can be no denying the fact that the psychological tone of the market is
strongly influenced by the level and direction of the stock market averages.

An analyst from the Lipper organization, appearing on CNBC, presented a chart that plotted fund inflow levels over a market cycle. The
inflows had increased as the market moved up to its top, but were transformed into outflows as the market approached its bottom, confirming the
influence of market psychology.

From a contrarian point of view, heavy fund inflows may well signal
that both the stock market averages and individual stocks could be getting
overextended. Conversely, outflows may be a signal that stock prices could
potentially become more attractive.

One approach to assessing the state of the market can be derived from
the investor's investment candidate prospect list. As has been suggested,
this list should be continually updated and monitored. Invariably, the num-

ber of attractive investment candidates tends to decline dramatically when stock market valuations are too high. But once that prospect list expands and contains more than a handful of serious investment candidates, this may signal an improving buying opportunity.

During the bubble phase of the market, nothing made much sense. In "Rationality vs. the Market," the following examples indicated the disconnect that often occurs between stocks and the averages:

> The DJIA was up approximately 24% in 1999, and yet almost 2 of 3 of NYSE listed stocks were down for the year.
>
> The S&P 500 index was up approximately 20% in 1999, and yet 25 stocks provided the entire gain for the index with the other 475 stocks averaging no gain at all.

During much of 1999, investors who chose not to speculate in momentum stocks could not help but feel left behind as their own stock holdings significantly lagged the popular averages. But what transpired during and after the bubble made the huge difference between investing and speculating abundantly clear—a lesson that investors will hopefully not quickly forget.

Investors are often reminded that over the longer term and across various market cycles, the stocks that they choose to invest in matter much more than the performance of the market averages—which is obviously a valid observation. But that does not obviate the fact that there may be times when one should be underinvested or even completely out of the market, and the action of the "averages" can provide a compelling case for reaching that conclusion.

The stock market, as reflected by the major averages, can be exceedingly fickle and hard to comprehend at times, requiring the investor to strictly adhere to established basic principles. For much of the year following September 11, the major averages experienced sharp daily advances and declines, making it difficult for individual investors to interpret, for example, the implications of a 500-point gain in the DJIA that was quickly followed by a 300-point decline. One day's euphoria based on an analyst's blanket "buy" recommendation for tech stocks would be transformed into despair as sales and earnings expectations were lowered by a high-profile company on another day. It seemed as if the "stock market" was grasping at straws on any given day—and drawing cosmic conclusions about future prospects for stocks, the economy, and the market.

There are, however, two aspects of the major averages that deserve particular scrutiny:

1. Trend and technical condition
2. Valuation levels

In spite of the distortions inherent in the major averages that were previously discussed, the underlying trend of the averages clearly provides a reflection of general investment sentiment. And when that sentiment is considered along with the technical condition of the averages, investors are in a better position to draw the appropriate conclusion.

As has been amply demonstrated, valuation eventually does matter for stocks—and the levels of the major averages should not be exempted from that basic rule. In spite of glib Wall Street, Inc. projections for ever-higher DJIA and S&P 500 levels, it would seem difficult to justify higher averages from a valuation point of view if the stocks in the indices are themselves overvalued.

The Nikkei got grossly overvalued in the late 1980s at a level close to 40,000, but in mid-2002 it traded as low as 9500. This is mentioned not to compare the two markets, but to note that market averages can reach unrealistic levels and become overvalued because of unjustifiable valuations of individual stocks.

Valuations for the major averages like the DJIA and S&P 500 should always be an issue and a consideration, but this is particularly true at P/Es of 25 or more. Even more scrutiny and attention should be directed at the nonexistent P/E of NASDAQ.

It is interesting to note that in a bull market, Wall Street, Inc. emphasizes how well the "stock market" is doing—which, of course helps generate investor enthusiasm and eagerness to invest in the Street's recommended stocks. But when the stock market takes a turn for the worse, investors are informed that the stock market has actually degenerated into being a "market of stocks."

The fact of the matter is that investors should always think in terms of a "market of stocks" because it places the primary emphasis where it belongs—on individual stocks.

However, in a revealing example of Wall Street "think," an investment strategist appearing on a financial network program suggested the purchase of S&P 500 index vehicles—because under the market conditions existing in mid-2002, he felt that it was exceedingly difficult to make investment decisions on individual stocks. In other words, since stocks were apparently overvalued or risky, his solution was for investors to bet on the stock market averages. What simply amazing logic and advice!

4

THE ELEMENTS
OF DEVELOPING
A STRATEGY

T
he value of having reviewed the distinctly different market periods since 1950 and then reevaluating investment principles and
guidelines is that this process provides some degree of perspective relative to the task of developing an effective strategy and
approach to investing.

Investors are often advised that since it is impossible to time the market, shareholders should remain fully invested at all times. Advocates of
that approach implicitly emphasize the opportunity for gain that the stock
market assuredly provides. However, one need only revisit the 16-year jour-
ney to nowhere during the 1966 to 1982 period and the more recent collapse of the Internet bubble to understand that the concept of stock market
risk cannot be totally ignored. There can be no denying that in making the
decision to invest or not to invest in stocks, investors should understand and
carefully consider several prominent potential risks.

Risk: Market, Industry, Company, General

Market Risk

One recurring market risk results from the underlying cyclicality of the economy. If the Federal Reserve decides, for example, that the economy is heating up, it may well apply the monetary brakes to slow economic activity. If it goes too far in that direction, the danger is that the economy could slip into recession, hurting corporate profits, which in turn puts pressure on the stock market.

There are also exogenous factors that cannot generally be predicted— like the 1973 oil embargo, the Gulf War, or the September 11 attack—that can affect the stock market to varying degrees. The dramatic increase in oil prices after the oil embargo had a profound impact on the economy for the better part of a decade, resulting in high rates of inflation, stifling interest rates, and a difficult stock market environment. The Gulf War generated a sharp but fairly temporary market reaction. While the September 11 episode shocked the nation and took its toll on the economy, it remains to be seen how lasting its impact will be.

For the most part, the 1982–2000 period was characterized by an economic background that seemed to suggest that economic growth and improving prosperity would continue indefinitely. The collapse of the Internet bubble and the September 11 episode have both served to temper that outlook by reintroducing the concern about market risk.

Industry Risk

As previously mentioned, industry selection is very often pivotal to investment success. Beyond the normal cyclicality experienced by certain industries, the matter of more fundamental problems affecting particular industries deserves close attention. For example, the condition of the telecom industry contains risk not only for the companies in that industry, but also for their suppliers. In addition, large bank loans to those companies, to failed companies like Enron, and to "problem" countries could present potential problems for the large money center banks.

Prudence would suggest that investors concentrate on industries that have either favorable or improving prospects.

Company Risk

There are certainly quite a number of company-specific risks to con-sider—but fortunately, a thorough review of the company's business and financial performance and an acquaintance with its product lines, cus-tomers, and competitors should go a long way toward assessing the "risk quotient" of a given company.

The one great intangible about a company, however, is the quality of management. Unfortunately, it is nearly impossible for individual investors to gain access to the management of large companies, and so one can only make inferences based on the company commentary contained in news releases and annual reports.

While fair disclosure (FD) regulations restrict CEOs and CFOs from discussing details that have not been publicly disclosed, management con-tacts at small and midsized firms can sometimes provide the individual investor with worthwhile insights. Investors should also take advantage of quarterly online conference calls in which management discusses the com-pany's earnings releases and takes questions from analysts. Since any com-ments made by management on these conference calls are considered to constitute publicly disclosed information, management is at liberty to answer all questions as straightforwardly as it desires. How the managers answer particular questions may provide a good indication of how forth-right management really is.

General Investment Risk

Investment risk always lurks in the shadows in one guise or another—it is just a matter of "how big a risk." With the stock market attempting to overcome the significant damage inflicted on the major averages in the aftermath of the bubble, the question on everybody's mind is, "Now what?"

The great dilemma, then, is whether the stock market is really as attractive at current levels as the congenital optimists on Wall Street seem to suggest.

The arguments emanating from the same group of investment strate-gists that helped foster the recent bubble is that the market correction has run its course, primarily because of the combination of the Federal Reserve's aggressive interest-rate cuts, which dropped Fed funds rates to a 40-year low, and lower tax rates—thereby assuring the start of a new bull market.

But something doesn't seem to ring true about that thesis. To begin with, the average market multiple over the last several decades has been only about 14, so why is the market so undervalued with P/Es in the mid-20s? Second, with long-term GDP growth estimated at 3.0 to 3.5 percent annually, how can corporate earnings grow faster than 8 to 9 percent? And how does that level of earnings gains support such lofty P/E values?

The critical question for the average investor, then, is do you buy into the Wall Street view that stocks are basically cheap at these levels, since most investment guidelines suggest otherwise. But the more important issue arises in trying to answer the question of what specific stocks to buy, and why.

That is where the real disconnect comes into play. Abby Joseph Cohen of Goldman Sachs, like other investment strategists, makes her periodic pronouncements about the "market"—meaning the DJIA and the S&P 500—but refrains from being specific about which stocks to buy. That task is left for the analysts, who conveniently are anxious to tout their list of stocks that will surely benefit from the expected upward thrust in the market that has been projected by none other than the firm's strategist.

In a market environment in which a number of thoughtful and responsible stock market veterans like Warren Buffett and John Bogle expect an extended period of subdued market performance, investing may get even more challenging. If Buffett and Bogle are correct, investing may also get to be frustrating as well as challenging. Operating in that environment will call for even greater discipline.

It is with that in mind that the following elements of a strategy are presented. The elements basically constitute a checklist of rules and considerations that might serve to suggest possible avenues of investigation or research regarding specific situations. The list is intended to give individual investors a starting point for establishing their own personalized checklist.

Investing is certainly more than a sporting game, but one comparison to sports illustrates an important aspect of the elements of a strategy. In both football and basketball, for example, the function of a coach is to call particular plays in particular situations. In essence, winning games depends upon having an adaptive and multidimensional array of options.

The decision to pass, run, or kick a field goal in football, or to drive to the basket or try a 3-point shot in basketball, depends on a number of considerations. The same logic applies to choosing between the options presented in the elements of a strategy—leaders versus laggards, growth versus value, diversification versus concentration, and so on. The checklist should be utilized much like a coach's play list—calling the right play at the right time, as dictated by the situation.

Leaders, Laggards, or Out-of-Favor Stocks

The concept of investing in market leaders has long been advocated by the investment community, and it often makes good sense. That philosophy, however, has at times been distorted by the professionals as they engaged in the "momentum" style of investing—buying stocks that are demonstrating strong relative strength because of buying by other big money players. That was the case with Cisco (CSCO), for example, which was featured as a "must own" stock by every analyst who appeared on CNBC, in spite of a fantasy-level P/E valuation.

When Cisco was really bubbling in early 2000, I met an ex-CEO who had retired after his NYSE-listed company was acquired by a larger firm. We both were waiting to board a flight from Maui to the big island of Hawaii. He had just called his Chicago-based money manager, and the news was just great—Cisco had closed up $3 per share for the day.

At the time, my own investment in M/I Schottenstein Homes (MHO), a homebuilder, which could have been classified as both a laggard and badly out of favor, was not doing well at all. But a role reversal between the performance of CSCO and MHO began to develop during the next few months. I often wonder whether that ex-CEO's money manager, and so many others like him, were able to get their clients out of CSCO at reasonable prices.

This example supports the case for both strategies. It is, however, a matter of good timing. Cisco had a great run, rewarding those who followed the leader, up to a point. But as Warren Buffett would say, valuation eventually does matter.

Growth versus Value

Growth stocks sometimes tend to have a "nifty-fifty" aura about them. A more recent variation of the growth style of investing supports growth, but at a reasonable price (GAARP). That sounds like a very prudent philosophy, but some managers seem to stretch the bounds of reasonableness implicit under GAARP by asserting that three times the growth rate is acceptable.

The term *value stock* is often a shorthand way of defining a low-P/E stock with unexciting growth prospects. The key for the investor, of course, is to capitalize on significant changes that could alter that image, as happened with Hadco and MHO—both of which were transformed into what could be termed "value growth stocks" by virtue of rapidly expanding earnings.

Asset Allocation

The matter of asset allocation is a question of both diversification and a suitable balance between current income and potential capital gains. The fairly typical 50-50 split between stocks and income-oriented investments can be adjusted according to age, risk tolerance, and general market conditions.

Most individual investors, however, have the flexibility to quickly and dramatically reduce their stock holdings, and even get completely out of stocks, when that course of action is indicated. Conversely, a more fully invested position can be readily established as conditions and opportunities warrant.

An interesting asset allocation option involves preferred stocks that trade on the exchanges and pay a stated level of interest or dividends each quarter. These two features of preferreds seem somewhat advantageous relative to bonds, which pay interest every six months and are often somewhat difficult to buy or sell. And with yields in the 7 to 9 percent range, preferreds would seem to deserve serious consideration in the asset allocation mix.

One particular group of preferreds that has not attracted much general notice is bank preferred stocks. Basically, banks that issue so-called trust preferred stocks derive a tax advantage in that the interest or dividends are paid on a before-tax basis. An additional benefit is that the banks can include a portion of the proceeds from the initial offering as part of their capital base. Based on these advantages, a growing number of banks are issuing trust preferred stocks.

These 30-year instruments are issued at a face value of $25 per share and are callable any time after 5 years at the issuer's discretion. From a practical point of view, however, since these instruments are an important part of the institution's capital structure, they will be called only if they can be reissued at more advantageous interest rates. It is because of this call provision that these preferreds tend to trade at close to their $25 par value. This relative price stability as compared to that of long-term bonds can be important to many income-oriented investors.

Another attractive feature of bank preferreds is that they have been issued by a number of regional banks that rely primarily on savings and mortgage activities, making it possible to assess their financial strength and risk profile much more readily than would be possible for other issuers like larger money center banks or certain other corporations.

Big Cap versus Small Cap

To begin with, big-capitalization stocks provide the level of liquidity that fund managers feel comfortable with. But at times that preference can be overdone. As indicated in Table 2.2, just 22 technology stocks had been driven to a peak combined valuation of $4.77 trillion. An example of the concentrated trading in these stocks can be assessed by the fact that when Cisco traded 100 million shares at a price close to its high of $82 per share, its dollar trading volume for the day amounted to about $8 billion. The funds could easily move that amount of money into Cisco because of its approximately $600 billion valuation, but such large amounts of money could not be put into small-capitalization companies without dramatically affecting their prices.

The dilemma for the individual investor is that this decided preference for big caps on the part of money managers means that there is generally little or no institutional sponsorship or analyst support for even potentially interesting small-capitalization stocks—in which case these stocks may well languish until the institutions change their strategy.

One such shift in strategy did, in fact, occur starting in early 2001 as poorly performing technology and other big-cap stocks took their toll on the performance of mutual funds and forced a number of money managers to revisit the small-cap part of the market. And with their buying power, they succeeded in easily and dramatically moving a number of previously dormant stocks. The obvious next question, of course, is how quickly they will sell the small caps when they revert back to their normal preference for the big caps.

The underfollowed small-cap part of the market can, nevertheless, provide some unusually promising prospects. An example of how research and analysis in this area can prove to be rewarding is exemplified by Tractor Supply Co. (Figure 4.1). The stock bottomed in late 2000, coincident with the NASDAQ meltdown. With the big-cap game under attack, funds began to shift to other parts of the market.

At its low, Tractor Supply (TSCO) was really a micro-cap stock, valued at about $60 million. The P/E level had approached 5 times earnings, providing further evidence of how distorted the market's perception had become during the bubble phase.

FIGURE 4.1   Tractor Supply Price Chart

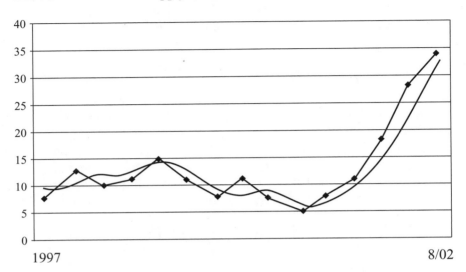

The action of TSCO as captured by its chart provides further validation of the value of using moving-average lines for technical analysis. After crossing the 100-day moving average line, the stock continued to trade above that line during a sustained upward move.

Diversification versus Concentration

Just about all professional advisers will stress the importance of diversification, but relative concentration may make good sense under the right circumstances. The significant discrepancy noted in Table 3.7 between the performance of the top third of the Dow stocks and that of the middle and bottom thirds tends to support the case for some measure of concentration.

It goes without saying, however, that the potential for increased risk in a concentrated portfolio must be matched by an accompanying heightened sense of concentration on the analytical side of the equation.

One of the main advantages attributed to mutual funds is the relative protection inherent in a widely diversified portfolio. In fact, this principle has been carried a step further by the concept of a "fund of funds."

There is no question that many investors have not felt inclined to get involved in stock selection, and as a consequence find comfort and convenience in mutual funds. However, selecting from among 8000 mutual funds is in many respects just as daunting a task as selecting individual stocks. Compounding the mutual fund selection problem is the fact that last year's outperforming fund can often be this year's laggard. Mutual fund investing is ultimately based on the expectation of favorable market conditions and faith in the fund manager.

As the market declined following the September 11 episode and the corporate accounting scandals, many large-capitalization stocks were severely punished, and mutual funds basically had nowhere to hide—and so despite their broad diversification, the performance of mutual funds essentially mirrored that of the market.

The polar opposite to diversification, of course, is following a more concentrated approach to portfolio selection. In spite of the risks, there are certain circumstances under which a concentrated portfolio can produce extremely rewarding results.

This brings to mind a stock that by today's standards was "value-plus." In early 1975, I was attracted to United Financial (UFL) by its book value of $19 per share and estimated EPS of $2.20 for 1976—and its $6 per share stock price. I had been on the company's mailing list based on an earlier request, and I was increasingly impressed by the apparent quality of its management team. The officers and directors had been active in the S&L business for many years, and the copies of speeches and presentations that they made to the banking and investment community convinced me that the company's prospects were quite good—which resulted in a decision to buy the stock.

Even though the stock market moved up rather strongly in the next few months, the price of UFL did not budge. Based on indications that the company remained on track to meet the earnings level that I expected, I bought more stock and wrote a letter to the chairman suggesting that, under the circumstances, the board should consider a stock repurchase program. A courteous reply thanked me for my interest and indicated that the board periodically reviews such matters.

Shortly thereafter, in what seemed to be an incomprehensible development, a Boston-based mutual fund sold a 500,000-share block to the company at $5 per share. At that point it became clear that the fund's large block of stock had been overhanging the market, putting pressure on the stock's price. What makes that transaction even more bizarre is the fact that a year later the same mutual fund bought back the same amount of stock on the open market at $12 per share. The company proceeded to report a $2.30 EPS for 1976, $3.22 in 1977, and $3.89 in 1978 before announcing a merger agreement in mid-1979.

Maybe it is the type of investment decision making exhibited by the fund that sold its UFL holdings at $5 per share that has brought into question the investment acumen of mutual fund managers, then and now, and has served to popularize index funds.

For the most part, individual investors can count themselves fortunate to have generated and capitalized on just a small number of what can be deemed great investment ideas over the years. So when one of these situations seems right, and you have investigated the company and its fundamentals as thoroughly as possible, relative concentration may be in order.

A critical rule of investing is to establish a well-thought-out standard of evaluation and to follow it. This discipline is essential in distinguishing special situations from more problematic or speculative ones.

Following that approach during the Internet craze of the 1990s could have saved many investors from buying into supposed opportunities of a lifetime that ultimately turned out quite badly.

Buy a Company, Not a Tip: Understanding Company Dynamics

Stories abound about investors who bought stocks on the basis of tips and lost heavily. Since the original source and the basis of a particular tip usually cannot be ascertained, tips should be avoided and assumed to be suspect unless proven otherwise after following the rigorous rules of fundamental and technical analysis.

Warren Buffett's investment approach essentially asks the question, would you buy the company based on a thorough understanding of its business and its financial condition? The Gorman-Rupp Co. (GRC) example is interesting from a number of perspectives. To begin with, the company, which manufactures a wide range of pumps, has exhibited steady revenue growth to the $200 million level. And it has done this while increasing its dividend payout ratio to approximately 38 percent and maintaining a debt-free balance sheet and a $20 million cash-equivalent position.

Gorman-Rupp's 5-year income and balance sheet statements are summarized in Tables 4.1 and 4.2. These statements have the important virtue of transparency, and, more important, they do add up, as determined by the close correspondence of retained earnings each year to increases in reported stockholders' equity. Retained earnings in this instance are defined as

Retained earnings = income − dividend payout − stock repurchases

Table 4.1   Gorman-Rupp 5-Year Income Statement Summary

	Sales ($ millions)	Income ($ millions)	Profit Margin	EPS	Dividends per Share
1997	165	10.6	6.4%	1.23	0.56
1998	171	11.8	6.9%	1.37	0.58
1999	179	13.1	7.3%	1.52	0.60
2000	190	13.8	7.3%	1.61	0.62
2001	203	14.6	7.2%	1.70	0.64

Table 4.2   Gorman-Rupp 5-Year Balance Sheet Summary

	Current Ratio	Stockholders' Equity ($ million)	ROE
1997	4.8	78.1	13.5%
1998	4.5	83.7	14.1%
1999	4.8	92.3	14.2%
2000	4.3	100.0	13.8%
2001	4.9	107.9	13.5%

GRC's balance sheet is as clean as a balance sheet can be—it has an excellent current ratio with receivables and inventories under great control, along with the absence of any debt. There are no "Accounting in Wonderland" or goodwill issues to complicate GRC's financial statements. When evaluating other companies' statements, the question to ask if the numbers don't add up in some comprehensible way should be, what am I missing?

It is almost axiomatic that if companies are to survive and thrive over the long term in a competitive environment, they must, in one way or another, strive to reinvent themselves. In some instances the changes may be slow and evolutionary, but in other cases companies often take sudden and dramatic steps to enhance their prospects for growth.

These efforts reflect management's recognition that there is such a thing as a company's life cycle. Every company is subject to changes in market preferences for different products, and if the company doesn't adapt quickly enough, it may soon find itself at a serious disadvantage. That has happened to so many companies—Polaroid, for example. Polaroid was basically a one-product company participating in a shrinking market, and it had been obvious for quite a while that its company dynamics were not encouraging. In fairness, management did embark on a number of costly new product development programs, but unfortunately, most of them failed to meet expectations.

Some prominent examples of companies whose prospects dazzled investors before they ultimately succumbed to the competitive pressures of the marketplace include names like Wang Laboratories, Prime Computer, Digital Equipment, and Data General.

The life cycle of Wang Laboratories was similar to that of Polaroid, but much shorter. Wang gained early dominance in the word-processing market of the 1970s, but it was not able to capitalize on its position before word-processing capabilities were integrated into the newly introduced PCs. Part of that failure could possibly be attributed to the fact that voting control of the company was held by the founder and his family. When the elder Wang decided to step aside from the management of the company, he installed his son as president at what turned out to be a very critical point in the company's life cycle.

Prime, Digital, and Data General had been significant beneficiaries of the transition from large mainframe computers to minicomputers, but they basically missed the rapid transition from minis to PCs. In these instances, the life cycle factor affected both the companies and a whole industry.

For the investor, it is important to identify a company's vision for its future. In some instances, companies establish a pattern of mergers or acquisitions as a vehicle for growth and product diversification. This frequently happens in the technology and drug sectors. In other instances, the motivation is geographical expansion and improved efficiency, which is often cited by banking and retail companies.

Of course, there is much to be said for the well-implemented plans of internal growth that characterize so many companies, such as Home Depot and Wal-Mart.

In essence, if the company's strategy and dynamics are not clearly identifiable, the basis for making reliable earnings projections may come into question.

Taking Profits

Some investors are prone to take profits too soon, while others often wait too long and let their potential gains slip away. It can be just as discouraging to sell prematurely as it is to have ignored the warning signs of a stock's topping action.

To a considerable extent, both situations are probably influenced by the ideas of "locking in" a good profit, on the one hand, and "letting the profits run," on the other, as opposed to relying strictly on fundamental and technical analysis to help make those decisions.

In some instances, the fact that a stock has experienced a significant appreciation should not necessarily trigger a sell decision. In fact, in the Hadco case, the brokerage houses did not issue their "buy" recommendations until the stock had doubled in price.

In addition to other general analytical factors, investors must decide whether the stock's current valuation remains compelling enough to attract other investors.

At times, investors can be caught off guard by some unexpected development in the form of the release of bad news about a company or an industry. There is an adage about stocks that warns that the first piece of bad news will very likely not be the last. As a consequence, the investor must exercise a high degree of objectivity, rather than being lulled into wishful thinking.

Obviously, care should be taken not to overreact to every piece of news. A good test in such instances would be to ask whether the stock is still a good buy, all things considered. But if there are lingering doubts, taking profits should definitely be a serious option.

One issue about taking profits is the influence of tax considerations. Waiting to take advantage of capital gains provisions can sometimes be rather costly. In one instance, I decided to wait another 3 weeks to qualify for a long-term gain—but the market had another agenda. Tax considerations also no doubt kept many investors from cashing out of some of their bubble high fliers at a price that would have yielded extraordinary gains—only to painfully watch as those huge paper profits were vaporized.

Research Checklist—
Validating Investment Candidates

An overall investment strategy is essential, but implementation of any investment plan involves much more specific detail. The following research checklist presents a series of items that are critical in establishing and validating individual candidates or in making buy-sell decisions. Investors are obviously encouraged to either choose from or expand the checklist to suite their own needs and preferences.

Any serious investment research effort on the part of individual investors depends in large measure on the indispensable resources available on the Internet. While the Internet bubble has burst, and the reputation of Wall Street, Inc. and the financial community has been severely tarnished—and the painful memories linger—the Internet itself can be viewed, without doubt, as an incredible technological achievement that has transformed the entire field of information technology.

The significance of the online financial data, interactive graphics, and screening tools available on the Internet is that individual investors now have convenient access to information in a way that could only have been imagined prior to the Internet, allowing them to efficiently and effectively develop a well-informed and disciplined approach to investment decision making.

In effect, the Internet, by basically eliminating the arduous and laborious manual data-gathering tasks that previously precluded most individual investors from conducting reasonably thorough research analysis, has empowered individuals with the ability to attain a much higher level of knowledge and understanding of the financial markets than would have otherwise been possible.

In building upon the significant advantage of having the vast information resources of the Internet so readily available, the questions for the individual investor become a matter of

1. What information is most relevant
2. Which combination of online sites can provide the desired data, research tools, and other pertinent information
3. How to correlate and evaluate that information in a systematic manner

The following checklist items attempt to address those matters.

Industry Sector Review

Two very informative and useful sources that investors can use to keep current about industry sector trends are (1) the *BusinessWeek* quarterly and annual corporate scoreboard issues, which compile industry sector data by aggregating sales and income results of the companies within each classification, and (2) the annual *Fortune* 500 and 1000 issue, which does much the same thing in a slightly different format. Both publications augment the data with a brief commentary on each industry and analysis of significant developments.

Certainly, the coverage of business news by both the *Wall Street Journal* and *Investors Business Daily* is informative, but it is the listings of reported company quarterly income results that should be carefully monitored. In addition to keeping track of companies of immediate interest, these listings can become the source of prospective investment candidates.

Investors should consider the practice of underlining the earnings reports of companies that seem unusually strong or weak as a means of developing a better insight into the underlying fundamentals affecting particular companies and their industries.

Web Site "Favorites" List

Of the many Web sites that provide business and financial resources, the following group—in the aggregate—should be adequate to serve the needs of most investors. While the sites provide similar information, some offer unique capabilities or variations in particular areas.

In that regard, it is difficult to rank them, but after exploring the features that each excels in, an investor will instinctively know which site to go to for a particular need.

yahoo.com, yahoo.marketguide.com, bigcharts.com, moneycentral.msn.com, bloomberg.com, investor.stockpoint.com, nasdaq.com, thomsonfn.com, quicken.com, money.cnn.com, stockcharts.com

Computer Screening Variables

Online computer screening capabilities provide an efficient method of identifying companies that satisfy certain prescribed financial limits. The variables listed here represent only a few of the standard financial measures that are often used in screening programs. By using appropriate upper and lower limits for each variable, the investor has the capability to define a ranked subset of companies that is as large or small as desired.

1. Market capitalization and price
2. P/E
3. Income and revenue growth rates
4. Price-to-sales ratio
5. Profit margin and debt-to-equity ratio

As a word of caution, it should be noted that the results of ranking routines can often be misleading because of the inclusion or exclusion of extraordinary items in the income level that is being used in the screening program's database. However, those instances should become readily apparent during the detailed fundamental review of each company's financial record.

Fundamental Company Analysis

Who can forget the admonition often stated by Ross Perot to "look under the hood," or his statement about how "the devil is in the details"?

Whatever opinion people have about Perot, his long years of experience in business are reflected in those pithy comments—and they are particularly applicable to the fundamental company analysis issues that follow.

1. 5-Year Income Statement and Balance Sheet Review

This should be the starting point of any company analysis. A fairly quick examination of income statements should reveal whether or not there is a consistency in the various components listed in the income statements—or whether certain items may be cause for concern. For example, a number of companies have been known to periodically record special charges in a given year that offset the previous year's income, resulting in basically no net earnings over an extended period of time.

If the balance sheet indicates a heavy debt burden or a high level of goodwill or intangibles, there may be reason to cut short any further analysis.

2. Profit Margin

Profit margins tend to fluctuate in a fairly narrow characteristic range, which generally reflects the nature of the company's business. For example, software and semiconductor companies normally tend to have very high profit margins, while retailers generally have very low profit margins.

As previously noted, an otherwise strong company with a depressed profit margin may provide an interesting potential investment if the stock price is valued to reflect the lower earnings, and if there are reasonable prospects that profit margins could rebound to more normal levels.

3. Return on Equity

This is a measure of how effectively a company utilizes its financial resources in its business. Typically, a 15 percent ROE is considered to be satisfactory, with 20 percent being above average and below 10 percent being considered subpar.

Warren Buffett has been a proponent of companies increasing their dividend payout to shareholders, which serves to reduce shareholders' equity and results in a higher ROE than would otherwise be the case. His thesis is that if the company cannot effectively maintain its ROE as equity increases, the company should distribute a portion of that equity to shareholders.

4. Relative P/E Valuation

Historically, the P/Es accorded to certain industry sectors will generally be at either a premium or a discount to the market multiple that exists for the DJIA or the S&P 500. This, of course, varies over time depending upon the changing industry fortunes brought about by business conditions.

The drug and pharmaceutical industry's P/E, for example, has consistently been significantly higher than that of the "market." However, that premium declined somewhat in 2002 because of concern about the inroads of lower-priced generics on the one hand, and adverse findings about the safety and efficacy of some new drugs on the other.

Another interesting valuation issue involves the question of how much investors should pay for a given growth rate. While it may be expected that all companies should be valued equally based on their apparent compound income growth rates (CIGRs), the market values a highly regarded company like Microsoft with a P/E well above its growth rate, while homebuilders, for example, sell at P/Es that are well below their long-term growth rates because of the perception that homebuilding is basically a cyclical business.

These general valuation factors have a certain validity to them, but they are not necessarily applied in a consistent or predictable way. Fortunately, it is that very market inefficiency that generates investment opportunities.

5. The Annual Report

While the sentiment expressed in some circles is that annual reports are public relations puffery, I nevertheless strongly suggest that investors request an investor relations package from companies of potential interest. These packages generally include the annual report, current news releases, and often the 10-Q and 10-K SEC filings, product information, and reprints of articles about the company.

These lengthy hard-copy reports are much easier to deal with than having to endlessly scroll through the online versions to find what you are looking for. Another advantage of a hard-copy report is that you can underline items that are of particular interest as you read the report—making it easier to develop a summary of positive or negative items of note.

6. Compare the Company Against Competitors

A company's prospects depend not only on its own strategy and actions, but also on those of its competitors. The classic cases that come to mind are Kmart versus Wal-Mart and Applied Micro Devices versus Intel.

That added competitive perspective may in some cases be enough to color the analysis of the company's past record.

7. Review the Company News Releases

Most Web sites list recent news releases for individual companies. In this age of fair disclosure (FD), companies are more inclined to release what may be regarded as material information. There are some developments that can significantly influence your assessment of the company's prospects, and you should make an effort to keep abreast of any such material disclosures.

8. Check Analysts' Recommendations, Earnings Estimates, and Ratings

While this item is at the bottom of the list for obvious reasons, there may be some information content to be gleaned from what analysts are projecting. However, that having been said, investors should be cautioned that many EPS estimates for companies that are listed online have been dramatically inaccurate and should not be accepted at their face value. For the most part, analysts tend to err on the side of optimism in their earnings forecasts, so when a projection for a particular company's EPS is unfavorable, it may be cause for second thoughts.

The Final Step: Risk/Reward
Trade-Off Analysis

The final step in the investment decision-making process involves making a clear-cut decision after assessing and evaluating the many variables that have been considered from both a fundamental and technical perspective.

Although investors are certainly well aware of general stock market risk, one critical mistake that should be avoided is the tendency to focus more on the reward potential than on the downside risk of particular stocks.

For example, when Cisco was hitting new highs at $82 per share, it was still being highly touted, even though its EPS was a lowly $0.36 per share. By any rational standard, anybody would have been hard-pressed to assign Cisco a further upside potential of 50 percent. On the risk side, however, since a 50 percent downside move would leave the stock still grossly overvalued, the risk/reward trade-off would certainly have gone against investing in Cisco at that price.

The virtue of including a risk/reward trade-off analysis in the investment decision-making process is to ensure that the investor is prepared when the risk factor becomes a reality—as happens when a newly purchased stock declines. In some situations, price declines can be an ominous foreboding of worse things to come, and may require a second look. But in other instances, a price decline may represent an opportunity to build a position in that stock at even more favorable prices.

In many cases, the stocks that produced some of my best long-term gains subsequently traded below my initial purchase prices. But because I had a strong conviction concerning their earnings prospects and the opinion that the stocks were undervalued even on current earnings, I was both willing and prepared to accept the possibility of a 10 to 20 percent price decline, and at times I initiated a scaled purchase of additional stock at preestablished price points.

Certainly, not all risk/reward trade-offs can be expected to produce conclusively black or white results. But even that fact conveys important information.

What is really indispensable about risk/reward trade-off analysis is the fact that it provides the discipline that helps keep an investor's emotions under control. All investors have at some time experienced a rush of enthusiasm about some particular investment idea, only to have either second thoughts or regrets. It is certainly better to have entertained the second thoughts earlier rather than later, and that is the purpose of risk/reward trade-off analysis.

Summing Up and Taking Stock

The DJIA broke the 1000 barrier in early 1966 and reached its all-time high of approximately 11,700 in early 2000—which equates to a 7.5 percent compound annual gain over a period of 34 years.

In sharp contrast, during the 5-year period between 1995 and 2000, the compound gains amounted to 46.5 percent for NASDAQ, 29 percent for the S&P 500, and 24 percent for the DJIA.

As a consequence of that extraordinary rate of growth, ever larger money inflows were required in order to move the markets and maintain such strong momentum. In that regard, a continuation of a 30 percent compound valuation gain over the 2000–2005 period would have implied an increase in total stock market valuation from its high of about $16 trillion to an incomprehensible level of $60 trillion. Obviously, that could not—and did not—happen. On the contrary, the bursting of the investment bubble subsequently chopped the valuation of the stock market to about $9 trillion in 2002.

As the major stock market indices declined to levels that confirmed the existence of a bear market, market participants began to focus attention on

1. How much lower the averages would go
2. The timing and strength of the prospective economic recovery

Those identical questions challenged investors in 1975 and 1982 as both the stock market and the economy struggled to recover. In those two instances, the stock market began to rally in advance of sure signs of economic recovery. However, it is important to note that stock valuations had been reduced to historic lows, with most stocks trading at P/E levels in the 7 to 8 range.

With post-bubble valuations actually higher than long-term average levels, however, it may be prudent to allow the stock market's technical action to confirm a successful bottoming process, which would be indicated by a reversal in the slope of the 100- and 200-day moving averages from negative to positive.

When that happens, it is very likely that both market psychology and optimism about the economic outlook will be on the rise, potentially presaging the prospects of extended stock market gains.

While waiting for that eventuality, which can materialize rather unexpectedly, investors should continue in their efforts to prequalify potential candidates as thoroughly as possible, using time-tested principles and guidelines, while maintaining a high level of investment discipline at all times. In the final analysis, there is something to be said for the fact that good things tend to happen when preparation meets opportunity.

Index

About the Author

Fred Plemenos has an engineering degree (MIT) and a business degree (Northeastern University). He developed the Data-Outlook financial publication, became institutional research director of a small brokerage firm, and later joined Data Resources, Inc., to create the DRI Industry Financial Service that served both money management and corporate clients. He also served as a corporate director, and has been quoted in the *Wall Street Journal, Barron's, Fortune, BusinessWeek,* and other financial publications.